MW00995638

Bost

Me
Dad
Mark 9th at 5.18 .M.,

avis Sandro

ulations

The

at 5.40 .M.

e York Travis Sandwic

ongratulations On Yo

Splendid victory Co

Cambe

The Old Man

The Biography of Walter J. Travis

———◄•——•►———

Bob Labbance

Sleeping Bear Press

Sleeping Bear Press
310 North Main Street
P.O. Box 20
Chelsea, MI 48118
www.sleepingbearpress.com

Printed and bound in the United States.

10 9 8 7 6 5 4 3 2 1

Library of Congress Cataloging-in-Publication Data

ISBN 1-886947-91-0

Labbance, Bob.
The old man : the biography of Walter J. Travis / by Bob Labbance.
p. cm.
Includes bibliographical references.
ISBN 1-886947-91-0
1. Travis, Walter J. (Walter John), 1862–1927. 2. Golf course
architects—United States—Biography. 3. Golfers—
United States—Biography. I. Title.
GV964.T72 L32 2000
712'.5'092—dc21

00-009850

This book is dedicated to my family for their perpetual understanding, and to Geoffrey Cornish, Sydney Stokes, and Herbert Warren Wind—three gentlemen who, through their decades of professional encouragement, have been like family to me.

Acknowledgments

First of all, as with any project, this would not have been possible without the help and understanding of my wife Kathie and my kids Griffin and Simone—who will probably always wonder why I'm such a nut about taking on such huge projects. Secondly, this book would not have been as interesting without the invaluable help of Ed Homsey of the Walter Travis Society who tracked down minute data, organized the accumulation of graphics, and provided support and encouragement at the other end of e-mail, especially during crunch month. I also genuinely appreciated the help of "Winkie" Roessler—what fun it has been to get to know her and have a real connection with Walter J.

Thanks also to Syd Stokes, historian at Ekwanok, a great fan of Travis and a gentleman I am honored to call a friend. Also to Herb Wind and Geoff Cornish, two wonderful men who have supported and encouraged me for 15 years.

We're fortunate to have two great golf libraries in the U.S., and both the USGA Golf Library and the Ralph Miller Golf Library provided fantastic support. Thanks to Rand Jerris, Andy Mutch, Patty Moran and Nancy Stulack at the USGA, and Saundra Scheffer and Marge Dewey at Ralph Miller. Not to mention the immense help the personal library of Brian Siplo was, and his assistance with images and collateral material were invaluable.

Also thanks to Pat White, Tom Kuhl, Bob Kuntz, Pete Georgiady, David Cornwell, David Kriksceonaitis, Rees Jones, Don Brodie, Tom Doak, Ian Andrew, Maxine Bigliati, Rex Johns, Dave Homsey, Pat Oldis, Elwyne 'Sam' Palmer, Andrew Kliner at After Image, Johnny Paulk, Davis Love, Larry Startzel, Sid Matthew, Archie Hood, Mike Killian, Armand LeSage, Chris Dachisen, Lee Bowden, Jeff Roy, Doug Nunn, Rudy Fisher, Greg Searle, Jack Pascal, Bill Quirin, Tom Hamilton, Joe Donahue, Kevin Mendik, David Little, Tom Snodgrass, Randy Shaw, Dr. John Gershey, Joe Alonzi, Jeff Alpert, Paul O'Leary, Lew Zande, J. Paul Leslie, Donald Cook, Karen Bednarski, George and Susan Lewis, Rich Wells, Dale Scharfer, Ken Kirby, Jeff Spagna, and Brian Lewis, Lynne Johnson, Jennifer Lundahl, and Danny Freels at Sleeping Bear Press. I'm sure there are others who I can't remember because my brain is too small. Thank you, too.

Introduction

It was 20 years ago when I first became aware of Walter Travis. In a quest to play all the golf courses in northern New England, I stumbled upon the Equinox Golf Links in Manchester, Vermont. By the time I had negotiated all the twisting, turning fairways, escaped from the multitude of deep sand bunkers and been mystified by the rolling, quirky putting surfaces, I was interested in discovering who was responsible for this fine test of golf. When I found out that golf course architect Travis was buried just a few hundred yards away from the Equinox and that he spent many of his summers at the venerable hotel, I went for a visit and started a dialogue with "The Old Man" that continues to this day. You should hear what he thinks about the game of golf at the turn of the twenty-first century.

At the turn of the last century, Walter J. Travis was an American golfing icon. He championed state-of-the-art equipment, including the center-shafted Schenectady putter, metal woods, and a 52-inch driver. He detailed plans for greens construction and maintenance two decades before the establishment of the USGA Green Section or the greenkeepers association. He developed a practice regimen and tournament schedule to peak for the major tournaments of his era. He won the U.S. Amateur three times—95 years before Tiger Woods met the standard—and beat men half his age in the process. He founded and edited the premier golf magazine of the time, and contributed seminal essays on rules, caddies, handicaps, courses, and techniques.

With so many accomplishments, it is surprising that Travis has not sustained an exalted position in the annals of American golf. Truth be told, Walter J. was not the game's most popular figure. Respected, yes, but a man as opinionated and vocal as Travis had many detractors. Fortunately, part of his legacy is irrefutable. He began designing golf courses before he had won his first Amateur and continued to within weeks of his death, 30 years later. At the outset, Tom Bendelow was the busiest architect in the business and cross bunkering was the accepted method of enhancing the difficulty of a layout. Travis moved the sand to the sides of the fairway and by placing the hazards laterally, opened a direct path to the green for the dub, while forcing the better ball striker to demonstrate more precision in their game. Instead of the pancake-flat putting green of the day, he added modulation to the surfaces and forced a study of the ground game. He developed interesting routing plans where no two consecutive holes played in the same direction, and the back-and-forth monotony of many of the era's courses was eliminated.

Unlike the designs that preceded his, many of The Old Man's courses still exist today. Most have undergone recent renovations to enhance their playability—in some cases, undoing the remodeling damage that had been done in the 1950s and 1960s. The Equinox, where I first became interested in Travis, is a perfect example. When Rees Jones modernized the layout in 1991, he rescaled it for today's players—adding bunkers where needed and larger greens to accommodate the volume of play it now receives. But he left the routing and the diversity of challenges intact, and paid homage to Travis by complementing his features and flow. Jones claimed that he merely completed the job that may have never been finished properly due to the Depression and Travis's death in 1927. I think even Walter would have approved.

When the Walter Travis Society contacted me about a book to pay tribute to The Old Man, I was thrilled to participate. I spent many hours pouring over Travis's personal letters, read dozens of articles he wrote, combed through daily newspaper accounts of his exploits, researched his childhood in Australia, and interviewed family members—all to understand the essence of the man and what he meant to golf in America.

I hope I have successfully conveyed that to the readers. But if not, grab your clubs and make arrangements to play the Westchester Country Club in New York, Country Club of Scranton in Pennsylvania, Hollywood Golf Club in New Jersey, Lookout Point in Ontario, or Ekwanok Country Club in Vermont.

Then you'll understand.

Contents

The Architect

The Old Man

The Biography of Walter J. Travis

———◆———

The Golfer

Australian Roots

On April 5, 1852, 20-year-old Charles William Travis—the son of Benjamin Travis, a cotton manufacturer of Manchester, England—left Liverpool bound for Australia. Travis carried a family surname with its origins in the Travers family of Mount Travers, County Lancaster, England and Monkstoun Castle, County Dublin, Ireland, dating to the early 1600s. Benjamin was a direct descendant of Archbishop Travis of the Chester Cathedral in Chester, England.

Charles William boarded the passenger ship *Anna* in search of gold in Australia and a new life of adventure. The four-month voyage to Port Phillip was arduous, but Travis arrived safely on July 27, 1852, and headed inland to the Tarrangower Diggings, where gold had been discovered and ambitious prospectors were staking claims while larger mining operations were also moving in and setting up shop.

The road between Castlemaine and Bendigo was littered with miners. By day, the countryside was teeming with activity; by night, clustered around campfires, the miners weighed their daily booty and spun tales about the riches of the land yet uncovered. In December of 1853, news of a great, undiscovered gold field near Mount Tarrangower drew miners westward, where they discovered a land of beauty in the hills around the distinctive forest-covered peak. Over 3,000 miners would arrive in less than two weeks to seek their fortune.

On January 29, 1854, the English traveler William Howitt wrote, "There is a new rush and a violent one. Thousands and thousands of people who have come up here from the Ovens are now off again, helter-skelter, down to a place called The Porcupine, from the Porcupine Inn, beyond Bendigo. These crowds will in less than a fortnight have traveled upwards of 300 miles after new rushes." (Before the new area had been formally settled, it was referred to as "The Porcupines.")

Charles Travis was one of those who settled in nearby Emerald Hill, and on July 5, 1855 he married Susan Ilett—a native of Cornwall, England who came to Australia in 1849 as a teenager—at St. Paul's Church in Melbourne. They had obviously been courting for a spell, for their first child, Charles William Jr., was born just five months later on the 12th of December.

Realizing the desire of the miners to establish a permanent town, government officials commissioned surveyor John Templeton to select a site in 1854. By 1856, the work was complete. The town was named "Maldon" by a transplanted Englishman, after a sister city in Essex, England. In 1858, the first elected council was installed and although upward of 20,000 miners had been attracted to the area, many followed the next big find to other areas, and in 1861 the permanent population of Maldon was noted as 3,334.

Walter John Travis was born on January 10, 1862, the fourth child, all boys, of Charles and Susan. From their marriage in 1855 until 1879, they would sire eleven children—seven boys and four girls—though four of the children would die as infants or before reaching their tenth birthday. Charles worked in various mining capacities during the 1860s and 1870s, first as a manager and shareholder in the Eaglehawk Limited Company, later as an engineer and engine driver for the Great Nelson Company. At the time, gold sold for £4 per ounce and managers of Travis's position earned approximately £3 a week.

In those early years Maldon had about 70 stone and brick buildings, 370 wooden buildings and nearly 400 tents. There were about 25 businesses, including ten hotels and two breweries. There was a public hospital, two common schools, a courthouse, a German association with clubhouse, a public bath, and extensive services for the miners, including 26 quart-crushing machines. Coaches ran daily to other towns including Castlemaine, where one could catch a train to Melbourne.

Young Walter John was slight of build with above average intelligence. He did well at the Denominational School on Church Street in Maldon, had a penchant for writing, and enjoyed many sports and outdoor pursuits. An entry in the *Biographical Encyclopedia* claims Walter "was educated at Trinity College, Melbourne, Australia, from which he graduated with a degree of Bachelor of Arts." But a check with the University reveals no record of Travis attending the University during that time frame. Perhaps the confusion stems from the fact that the Denominational School was part of Holy Trinity church.

As a youngster Travis enjoyed hunting and was known by his siblings to make his own bullets and head out in search of kanga-

The Denominational School Travis attended as a youth
(Courtesy of Maldon Historical Society).

roos or pelicans as targets. He played tennis and cricket competitively, but without substantial success—golf did not arrive in Maldon until several decades after Travis had left for America.

His first job was as a clerical worker with Dabbs and Company, a downtown Maldon grocer and hardware store. The company occupied various locations in Maldon and continually expanded the products they offered to the local citizens—and a store still bearing the Dabbs name operates today. But Travis enjoyed the outdoors and sought work in that environment, at one point shipping out to Berry Jerry Station in New South Wales to take a job as a sheepherder on a homestead of hundreds of acres with sheep, horses, and other livestock.

It was a blow to the family in 1880—with seven children in the household, ranging in ages from one to 25—when patriarch Charles William was killed in a mining accident at age 48. Travis was working 300 feet below ground with fellow miner James Currie, who gave the following account of the accident. "We bored two holes and fired

Travis was employed at Dabbs Hardware in his
hometown of Maldon, Australia
(Courtesy of Maldon Historical Society).

them, and had crib [a light meal] about half-past three. After crib we
started another hole and got down about six inches when the explosion occurred. Travis was holding the drill and I was striking. After I
recovered from the shock I struck a light, and found Travis had been
thrown backwards, and was lying dead." The doctor who arrived to
investigate noted, "The deceased was dead on arrival at the claim.
The chin was driven in and appeared to have received the chief force
of the blow, the neck was dislocated and probably the skull was
fractured as well. Death resulted from dislocation of the neck."

When Walter's only surviving older brother also died the following year, he became the 'father' of the family, especially to the
youngest of the children who were considerably his juniors. Ethel
Maud was the youngest of the Travis children, and when she was
10, she penned a letter to 27-year-old Walter. His reply included the
following passage: "You are getting to write real good. If you are
improving in everything else as well then I do not suppose I would
know you. I don't think you would know me at first. I know that I
have changed very much."

Travis' father was killed in 1880, while working this mine
(Courtesy of Maldon Historical Society).

Many years later, Ethel's grown daughter wrote, "Walter and
my mother were brother and sister, she being the youngest member
of the family. Their father died when she was just a baby, as she
never remembered him. So Walter was the 'father of the family.'
Even after he went to America he always sent her books, and in later
years *The American Golfer.*"

Travis helped out with the chores, including chopping wood to
heat the house. Many years later his uncle wrote him and, in part,
said, "Tom [his son and Travis's cousin] says he remembers you
cutting wood and cutting your foot. Says he supposes you have the
mark still."

Travis felt he could not make a substantial financial contribu-
tion to the family with the job opportunities in Maldon. He did not
want to work in the mines, as he witnessed the toll it took on his
father, and by this time, mine output was already on the decline. So,
in the early 1880s, while still a teenager, Travis joined McLean Brothers and Rigg, ironmongery merchants headquartered on Elizabeth

Street in Melbourne. McLean Brothers was a growing company with offices in Melbourne, Sydney, Adelaide, and London, and Travis enjoyed the work and life in the big city. He rose up the hardware company's ranks quickly and was able to send money home to his mother and the six siblings still in Maldon.

In 1885, McLean Brothers decided to open a New York office. Just 20 years past the end of the Civil War, America was now booming and McLean Brothers felt there was a market for the larger hardware and construction products they carried. Company vice-president Cooke—who was in charge of staffing the new office—was impressed by Travis, and after consulting with management, approached him regarding a position in New York. Eventually, they asked the 23-year-old if he would be interested in heading up the new outpost.

Life and Love in New York City

When Travis arrived in New York in 1886, he found a city ready to take its place as one of the world's commercial hubs. Travis took a room in a boarding house, but without family or friends for distractions, he threw himself into his work. For the first two years he kept his nose to the grindstone and dedicated himself to the success of the New York office. He began to make friends through business and the communal meals served in the boardinghouses he lived in on the Lower East Side.

In 1888, McLean Brothers asked Travis to return to Australia to organize and run the company's booth at the Melbourne Centennial Exhibition. His brother Herbert Alfred, who was 15 years old at the time, recalls, "I visited the Exhibition many, many times and I used to get the pass tickets through Walter."

Satisfied that his mother was getting along, Travis returned to New York when the Exhibition was through. That would be the last time he set foot on Australian soil, a fact lamented by Uncle William Ilett, who wrote him in 1924, "It would be nice to meet again—it is a wonder you never take a trip to Australia as it is not far now. Traveling is so quick compared to what it was years ago."

But Travis was enamored of New York in the 1880s and wanted to be an American. He felt Australia held little opportunity for him, and despite missing his family, he dove into his new life full speed ahead. Travis was swept away by the bicycle craze of the time, at first riding one of the unicycles that appeared on the scene, later trading the difficult-to-handle machine for one of the new "safety bikes" that inundated New York. Travis pedaled to work, on short trips around the metropolitan environment and competitively in amateur races. According to writer H.B. Martin, with the new bike Travis "took to wheeling with a renewed interest and saw to it that no one passed him on the road."

With his friends, Travis played tennis, went bird hunting, and headed out on fishing expeditions. At home, they played poker or billiards well into the evenings. He also drank whiskey and smoked big, black cigars. He was enjoying the benefits of New York City life and able to utilize a small amount of disposable income. The aver-

Travis (seated center) with his friends at Niagra Falls in 1886,
shortly after his arrival in the United States
(Courtesy of Jim Espinola).

age annual wage for an American worker in 1889 was just under
$400 a year. Travis was making $50 a week in the city, and $2,600
a year allowed him to live comfortably. He resided first at 20 East
9th Street, then by 1887 at 51 West 25th Street. He was a modern
single man, and enjoying it, until one day in March, 1889.

One of the companies that McLean Brothers did business with
was Bartlett Bent Jr.'s Safety Stove Warehouse, a business headquartered in Middletown, Connecticut, with an office at 238 Water
Street in New York. It was there that Travis first met Bartlett's daughter
Anne—a 26-year-old beauty with a ready smile and a pleasant personality. Travis was attracted instantly, for Anne was a breath of
fresh air compared to the formal, often haughty young women that
frequented the New York social scenes. Though Anne was interested
in Travis as well, she kept her ardor in check in the early going.

Travis first wrote a brief note to Anne on March 17, 1889. After a
somewhat encouraging reply from her, he wrote the first of nearly

100 courting love letters on March 24. It was addressed to "My dear Miss Bent" and read in part, "It was with a great deal of pleasure that I received your kind and yet unkind letter yesterday. Unkind in attributing to me thoughts connecting 'Pigs in Clover' with yourself and the country, and *kind* in forgiving me for the uncommitted crime— and for writing at all. What can I say to free myself from the awful and undreamed of charge I am now saddled with? A vivid recollection of another little episode is still so 'fresh' in my mind as to convince me of the utter futility of establishing my innocence—but it is hard, very hard, to remain silent when not guilty. *Supposing* now that I did associate you with the country. Well, what is more truly complimentary? Do we not find in the country that keen delight, that sense of rest and content in gazing at those objects of natural freshness and beauty which are lacking in "the busy haunts of man," where most everything looks dry, dusty and faded? Fresh as applied to you, my dear Miss Bent, would be apropos rather than otherwise."

Although Anne lived in Connecticut, her friend Miss Hall resided in New York, and Travis refers to her as he continues his letter. "I am very glad to learn from Miss Hall that we shall soon have the pleasure of seeing you again. We will endeavor to compensate for any lack of kind treatment that you may suffer whilst under Miss Hall's wing."

A month passed before the two would see each other again, but when they did, some of the formality that had characterized their first meeting was washed away. They spent some time together in the boardinghouse that Travis inhabited at 21 Fifth Avenue and at her home in Middletown. On May 2, Travis wrote Anne again, asking, "I wonder whether you feel in any way as I do at this moment. I should like to think that your thoughts do revert occasionally to No. 21, but it would be almost too much to expect that I am associated in any way with those thoughts."

Anticipating another visit on the 11th of May, Travis wished to go public with his feelings for Anne. Her father was ill at the time, and would pass away within a few months, so Travis wrote to Mrs. Bent on May 8. His letter read in part, "During the few most delightful days I spent in Middletown, it must have been apparent to you that my regard for Miss Bent was of more than an ordinary character. I freely confess that I entertain the deepest affection for your daughter, and under these circumstances I realize that it is due to you that I should frankly avow my feelings, with the view of securing your sanction and consent to my addresses."

Travis went on to inform Mrs. Bent that he was the manager of the McLean Brothers office in New York, stated his current salary, that his family was in good standing and that his intentions were honorable. Travis did not hide his feelings by saying he sent this letter, "With the profound hope that you will allow me the opportunity of seeking to win the love of your daughter, in whom my whole affections are centered."

Travis received the response he was seeking. After the next escapade with Anne, the tone of his correspondence changed. "My dear Miss Bent," became "My dearest Nan,"—a name he would use for her throughout their lives, and "Very cordially, Walter Travis" became "Yours and yours only, Walter." Travis would soon take his middle name in his correspondence and forever become "Jack" to his wife and very close friends.

In 1998, when Walter Travis's granddaughter Adelaide Travis Emory passed away, she donated to the United States Golf Association (USGA), the 100 letters that Walter wrote Anne during the summer and fall of 1889. Walter wrote Anne once, sometimes twice, occasionally three times a day—often pedaling his bicycle to the post office at breakneck speed so the letter would make the afternoon train and be delivered the same day or, at worst, early the next morning. Three trains a day carried the mail between the two locations and delivery was made in the morning and afternoon—all this service 111 years ago! Travis lived for her replies, crushed when she went more than a day or two without writing back to him. When he panicked he would resort to telegrams to get her attention. He craved her affection, begged for her time, and glowed in the aftermath of their rendezvous.

For a man seen as dour, abrupt, and serious for much of his public life, Travis was effusive, romantic, and smitten while courting Anne. He could write six pages about nothing more than how much he loved her, missed her and couldn't possibly wait until they were together again. The letters, however, reveal a great deal about the 27-year-old Travis.

He didn't have a very positive view of organized religion, making several disparaging remarks on the subject, but realizing he had no audience for such in Anne. He dangled a trip to Australia in front of her but there's no record of them ever going. Later, when the romance hit a brief skid, he threatened to go there for a year by himself. He hunted birds along the coast and had the spoils of his shoots sent to her home, hoping "it will not cause your cook to strike." He fussed over getting a good photograph of Nan, and was disappointed that a couple of sessions did not work out to her satisfaction.

He noted the receipt of correspondence from home, including letters from both his mother and his grandmother. But he also said, "I am rather hazy as to the exact identity of several of my relatives. Have hitherto taken little interest in knowing just how they are related when I have never seen them." Travis was also very clear about his national allegiance during this time period. "I am an American to all intents and purposes," he wrote. "Coats-of-arms and all that have no place in a country that professes democracy."

He talked of poker, whist, and cribbage with his pals, but criticized one friend for going "truant" by staying out all night. "I don't go in for that sort of thing—and it's rather late making a start now." He fed her love of candy, and then poked fun at her for it.

He wrote passages such as, "If you could only feel the spasmodic fluttering of the heart that has missed its mate, that throbs and yearns oh so wildly to be with you again." And, "I love you so much, Nan, that I can find no pleasure in anything outside of your sweet self. All my thoughts are of you, and I shall never be perfectly content or happy until I can call you my own dear wife."

By mid-May, 1889, Walter had proposed and Anne had accepted, but there were still problems. Walter wanted to get married right away; Anne wanted to wait until at least January, if not the following June. Travis found this interminable and a sign of her hesitancy; Anne hoped to enjoy the single life a little longer. When she mentioned this to Travis, he wrote, "Your last letter was nice, long and loving, but one thing seemed to be out of time—the reference to your having 'a good time before the fatal day draws near.' Somehow, spoken in such cold blood, as it were, it jars upon me. I am not only sorry, but am grievously pained that you should care to have other men make love to you, or even make a pretense of doing so."

This passage leads one to believe that Jack and Nan had already consummated their union before wedlock—Travis following in the footsteps of his father—though the evidence would not be as conclusive since Jack and Anne's firstborn did not arrive until a year-and-a-half after their wedding.

They contested the wedding date for the entire summer and into the fall. Since none of the Travis family would come from Australia and Anne's father had passed away in September, it would not be a large wedding, and Travis saw no reason to plan it endlessly while they lived apart. He was also hoping for a rather modest ceremony. "I am glad there is a chance of having a quiet wedding, as I don't like any splurge, dear, as you know. Those ostentatious affairs remind me of a rocket—there's a big blaze and then oblivion."

There was a hot debate over Anne's desire for a long summer visit with her sister in Buffalo. Travis couldn't bear to have her so far away; Anne not only wanted to go, but planned to stay for weeks, during which time they would not see each other at all. Despite all his admonitions and attempts at "guilt trips," she went anyway.

As a 26-year-old, Anne had already passed the age where most women of her time were married, so she wanted to enjoy her freedom as long as possible. It might appear that she held this carrot over his head, testing his resolve and devotion as long as she could. On July 15, he finally reached the core of the matter, writing, "It begins to look as if you are going to be the 'boss,' so I suppose I may as well reconcile myself to my fate."

Meanwhile, they continued to banter about other matters. Travis had grown a mustache, and it proved to be the subject of much debate. It would come and go over the years, as well as the full beard that first appeared in 1900.

Though content in his work, Travis was approached by R.H. Dana, a friend from Australia whose company was interested in establishing a branch in New York and was looking for a manager. "They have offered me this position," Travis wrote to McLean Brothers, "and have guaranteed for three years an additional $1,000 annually over and above my present salary, with all traveling expenses paid, and at the expiration of that term have expressed their willingness to enter into more liberal arrangements. With a keen appreciation of the consideration I have always received at your hands, however, and moreover fully believing that you will exercise the same kind of care for my interests in the future, I have declined this proposition. You will understand that this offer came to me wholly unsolicited from Mr. Dana." His also informed them that he intended to marry. It is unclear whether this elegantly veiled threat had the desired effect of raising Travis's salary or not.

Jack and Nan discussed where they would live, and Travis researched various locations around New York City, quoting prices that included a room and meals. He checked the better hotels in town, including the Brunswick, the Clarendon and the Westminster—where prices ranged from $56 a week for a parlor, bedroom, and bath on a prime floor, to $35 for a single room on a middle floor—and concluded: "I very much fear, Nan, that the hotel idea will have to be abandoned. There is no disguising the fact that I can't afford it. There may be other good hotels where the rates are more moderate, and with that end in view I shall pursue my inquiries further. But for the life of me I cannot see anything so very objectionable in a *first-class* boardinghouse."

When she expressed dismay at the prospect of living in such a public setting, Travis countered, "I have, like yourself, aspirations above a couple of rooms in a boardinghouse, but it's good philosophy—and a Christian duty too—to endeavor to be content with the situation." By fall, after advertising in the paper, he believed he had found the right room, with a shared bath right outside the door and a private table in the dining room. Most of their meetings took place in Middletown, Connecticut, with Travis traveling there by train on Fridays. With the lodging issue pending, Travis hesitated to make a decision without her input and encouraged her to come to New York.

In October, Travis took ill and it surprised him: "I always thought I was invulnerable, but I find I am only mortal after all. I have been under a cloud—no tobacco nor yet any coffee for three days!! Just fancy that! *Perhaps* I may swear off altogether." While that outrageous statement would never come to pass, Travis' illness provided insight into his work ethic. "I must confess my conscience pricks me when I stay away from the office so much."

On New Year's Eve, 1889, Travis wrote to his fiancé in front of the fire, anticipating their impending union. She had already shipped some of her possessions to New York, and was due on the morning train on New Year's Day. However, her mother had taken sick and she was considering delaying her departure, something that Walter had trouble understanding. She would arrive a day later, approve of the room Travis had secured and make final arrangements for their wedding back in Connecticut.

Walter Travis and Anne Bent were married in Middletown on
January 9, 1890—a quiet ceremony with Anne's family in attendance. Shortly thereafter, they left on a tour of Great Britain before
returning to New York City to start their married life together. After
a short time in a New York City boarding house, they bought a small
home in Flushing and moved there later in 1890.

Family Life in Flushing

By 1894 Travis had comfortably settled into family life in Flushing. His marriage of five years was strong, his daughter Adelaide was an active three-year-old, and his son Bartlett was born on February 26, 1894.

For exercise, Travis played tennis with his friends. For recreation, he went hunting for birds along the shore during the migratory season. He occasionally joined fishing expeditions to the north and west with his companions, and often engaged in card games in the evenings. Poker, whist, and cribbage were played on the trains, at the clubs, and in the home, and Travis fancied himself a competent opponent. He held court around the billiard table he had installed in his home, and many a late-night match was enjoyed with cigars and whiskey enhancing the confrontations.

In September, the family gathered up Anne's mother and returned to Middletown for the first visit to Anne's childhood home in nearly five years, showing off the newest family members to aunts, uncles, and cousins in Connecticut. Walter shepherded the family there and then returned to Flushing to work, expecting the family to follow him in less than 10 days.

In that brief time he wrote volumes to Anne, as he had during their courtship in 1889. "I hope you will have a good time visiting the scenes of your childhood," he wrote, though he seemed to miss her presence just as much as he had before their marriage. "Now, with such a keen appetite for your letters and filled with such a desire to have you come home, all in the face of nearly five years of married life, seems to me rather out of the usual run and is a matter that has got to be looked into. You will, I'm sure, agree with me, you cold-blooded creature who has no desire except to stay away longer, that it's perfectly ridiculous for anyone to feel like this. This is my seventh letter," he groused, "—two from you. Talk about women's rights!"

Though now in his early 30s, Travis was not afraid to try new activities. When confronted with his weekday absences with the boys at the nearby Niantic Club in Flushing where he was a member, Travis made a promise to his wife. "I'll join you in learning danc-

Travis with wife Anne Bent and son Bartlett (left, b. 1894) and
Adelaide (right, b. 1891) circa 1895.

Travis came to America as the New York office manager for McLean Bros. & Rigg, hardware merchants of Australia.

ing—as you prayed me to recently," he wrote. "And when we learn to do the thing properly we'll have a devil of a time, not letting a hop within 20 miles escape us. We will drink of the fountain of Ponce de León, old woman, and shake a leg with the best of 'em."

While there is no follow-up on Travis's dancing prowess, in the following letter of September 5, Travis tossed off a single line that was more prophetic than he or anyone else could have realized. "John is going to import golf here and we are going to play shortly," he wrote to Anne in a paragraph that started with a discussion of the best train schedule to New Haven and finished with, "Sarah has been chaperoning a lot of Sunday School kids to a picnic at Bayside."

There is no evidence that Travis acted upon this statement either in the fall of 1894 or during the entire season of 1895. His letters never mention it again and his own account of starting the game make no reference to play during this time, even though the New York metropolitan area was a hotbed of golf by 1895.

Part of the reason was his professional life. McLean Brothers and Rigg had originally asked Travis to head the New York office for the Melbourne, Australia-based hardware company. His role there had been successful and the new outpost had flourished, riding the American tide of expansion. He had fended off other professional offers and stayed with the company that sent him to the United States.

In 1895, they asked him to work from the London office, and so began a period of 18 months where Travis spent a great deal of time in England, with little time for recreation. Travis was a take-charge kind of guy and his management skills were needed in the United Kingdom where the hardware company was needing solid help, though Travis was reticent to leave his young family and social contacts.

Travis resided at the West End Lodge on Streatham Common where he rented a room from Auctioneer Henry G. Betts. Although he split his time between his boarding room and the McLean Brothers office at 11 Fenchurch Avenue, in his travels he noticed golfers on every public green space. The game was expanding in the United Kingdom just as fast as it was in the States, and when he received a letter from one of his compatriots back home, he realized he would need to try the endeavor to keep up with his friends. Members of the Niantic Club intended to start a golf club and Travis was not to be left out.

Golf at a Ripe Old Age

Many years later, when penning his autobiography for *The Ameri-can Golfer* he reflected, "I was in London in 1895-1896 and learned that the Niantic Club, a social organization in Flushing, Long Island intended starting a golf club. I was living in Streatham at the time and it was no uncommon thing to see bunches of golfers playing Tooting Bec and Mitcham and Wimbledon, but the game made no appeal to me; on the contrary, I am free to confess that I had mild contempt for it, inspired possibly by the garb of the players, for in those days men's togs ran to rather "loud" checks in knickers and flamboyant stockings and red coats. However, I realized that I would have to sink my prejudices and start in with the rest of the Niantic boys, so I equipped myself with a set of clubs and, with anything but pride, brought them over on my return. In the early part of 1896 the Oakland Golf Club of Bayside, L.I. was formed and in October I first knelt at the shrine of the Goddess of Golf...and ever since have been a devout worshipper of the Royal and Ancient game."

John H. Taylor had leased 111 acres of land of a Bayside estate named The Oaks and hired the New York-based Scotsman, Tom Bendelow, to stake a nine-hole course. This was one of the first of more than 400 golf courses Bendelow would plot.

Travis returned to Long Island in the fall of 1896, joined the Club and played his first game of golf shortly afterward on the newly formed Oakland course. Although his natural athletic inclinations helped Travis to negotiate the layout, he was not satisfied and commented, "I appreciated my comparative helplessness after a few attempts."

Nevertheless, Travis was a beginner among beginners and his record in that very first season was a harbinger of things to come. As Travis noted, "I must, however, have had some latent aptitude for the game, for within a month after hitting my first ball the most cherished of all my golfing trophies came my way—a pewter tankard, the first prize in the first handicap competition of the Oakland Golf Club. Of course anyone can win a handicap affair if his handicap is big enough, but it is worth recording that I never won a handicap event at any time when I did not have the best gross score."

In November, Travis was convinced to enter a competition at Van Cortlandt Park sponsored by John Reid of St. Andrew's (NY). Although he finished second with an 18-hole score of 110, he was hooked. The disdain he had felt for golfers, and the love of tennis, fishing, hunting, and swimming evaporated. He spent the winter of 1896–1897 immersed in the literature and lore of the game. "I first provided myself with all the available literature on the subject, and after digesting, as well as circumstances would allow, the various instructions laid down by the eminent writers, I endeavored to discover by practice which was as constant as I could make it, which particular method suited me best and which promised to yield the best results."

He concentrated on the words of Horace Hutchinson in the *Badminton Golf* book and Willie Park Jr. in his book *A Game of Golf*. He discarded much of the instruction of the day that was directed at the younger player with physical attributes he could never develop. Most of the golfing converts prior to the turn-of-the-century were young, active men with limber frames and still developing muscles. Many were teenagers who were long-winded, agile, and well-toned.

Travis was 35 years old in an era when few lived past 75. He was slight of physique, never cracking 140 pounds, short of stature, and he liberally indulged in long black cigars and high-proof whiskey. He was also a businessperson with multiple responsibilities and pressures; a family man with two young children and a spouse to support and nourish. He did not fit the golfing mode that the press was cultivating. The year prior, 19-year-old Horace Rawlings had won the first U.S Open, while college students battled for amateur titles.

He developed a style that suited his physical attributes and mental acuity. "This naturally involved an enormous amount of experimenting before any fairly well-defined style was finally evolved, but by no means was all this practice wasted," he wrote in *The American Golfer*. "It brought me to a knowledge of many ways of making the different strokes and producing the desired results, and, more important than this, it yielded me a clear perception of the true relation of cause and effect in golf. This is the most valuable information a golfer can possess, especially when all goes not well with his game. When I, in my own struggling way was suffering from topping, slicing, pulling and all the rest, or did any of the other hundred things which a golfer may do and be sorry for doing, it did not take me much time to discover the actual trouble, and then the remedy could be at once applied."

Travis absorbed the fundamentals, applied them to his abilities and then learned how to diagnose his own problems on the course and make mid-round corrections. He did it all without the help of a professional teacher, something that he considered a blessing. He reasoned that many of the teachers of the game were but youngsters themselves and fully able to demonstrate a smooth effortless swing—in part because they also commenced the playing of the game at a young age. "Slavish imitation hampers individualism," he commented. "No two men swing exactly alike."

At the urging of the neophyte membership, Oakland hired professional George Strath in April 1897, but Travis continued to work on his own game, concentrating on his swing throughout the late winter and early spring.

He also considered the Oakland course an excellent facility for his purposes. "The Oakland course lends itself admirably to the development of one's game," he wrote. "It is undulating, the undulations being on a broad scale, stopping short of being hilly, and with a glacial moraine running through part of it, from forty to eighty feet deep, faced rather steeply in places. This ravine furnishes a variety of hanging lies. Not only that, but if one failed to carry the ravine on the second shot to the 'Heavenly Twins' green the ball three times out of four would roll to the bottom, necessitating a high lofted approach to the green on the plateau above. It was a hard shot, for be it remembered we were then playing with 'guttie' balls which were much more difficult to 'get up' than their compeers of today; moreover, we were not then equipped with the niblick and mashie–niblicks with ribbed or scored faces of the present generation, which render the execution of such strokes comparatively easy.

"We had to get the ball up quickly seventy or eighty feet, the face being quite steep, and to stop it quickly to avoid going out of bounds, and this could be done only with the aid of a pronounced cut.

"Many and many an hour have I spent practicing the shot, and as a result I got so that I used to 'show off' a bit by pitching balls over trees and bushes twenty to fifty feet high within a yard or so of the base and landing them dead within the same distance on the other side. It was a 'stunt' that proved quite useful on many an occasion in actual play." (Clearly, Tiger Woods isn't the first to command the flop shot.)

When writing his autobiography for *The American Golfer,* Travis recounted this memorable event from that time. "On Lincoln's Day, in February, 1897, I took part in my first open competition, 18 holes handicap medal play, at the inaugural tournament of the Ocean County Hunt and Country Club, at Lakewood, New Jersey. There were two inches of snow on the ground and when the first pair drove off it was snowing heavily, followed by alternate bursts of sleet, rain and snow." Travis was told that "Snow Rules" were in effect, which translated to no rules for some of the players. That was the beginning of a dogged determination throughout his career to play the game by the official rules and to assure that others obeyed as well. It was a position that is standard today, but was not a popular path at the time.

He played but a few rounds in the early part of the season and quickly learned that he needed to alter his practicing emphasis. At first he disdained "such a trivial and unimportant thing as putting," preferring instead to spend long hours on the range, developing a driving style he could count on during competition. "At this stage my experiments were confined almost exclusively to driving and iron play generally, the gentle art of putting being left to take care of itself, with the result that for the first two or three years I was quite weak on the putting green."

Ready to test his game against the amateur competition, Travis filled the summer with tournaments. In May, still playing off a seven handicap, Travis rode his bicycle up to the first tee at the Meadow Brook Hunt Club and submitted his entry for the Hempstead Handicap Cup, despite never having seen the golf course before. The unknown Travis made the turn in 50 and then with one round's experience under his belt, blistered the nine-hole loop in 40 his second time out and tied with J.C. Rennard for low gross. He also established a new course record. The next day he completed the sweep by winning the play-off for low net.

A few days later, he won the club championship at Oakland with an 82. Less than a week after that, he captured the Knollwood Handicap Cup—a two-round event at the Knollwood Country Club where his 167 won low gross and the 161 which resulted from a six handicap captured the low net. He played well in an open scratch event at

Shinnecock Hills, but lost in a play-off for one of the 16 match play spots. In a consolation round that followed, he carded an 83—one of the best rounds of the tournament.

Travis characterized his successes as trivial, stating "The time now came when I was to see what sort of stuff I was made of at match play. A man may be good at the score game and yet comparatively weak at match play. To prove of sterling worth a player must be strong at both forms of the game...that is the acid test."

Travis chose the first meeting of the Norwood Park Field Club at Long Branch, New Jersey in August for his personal test of mettle. He was second to W. Girdwood Stewart, a visiting Troon player in the qualifying and the two would meet in the final. To get there Travis disposed of H.P. Phillips 5 and 3, D.W. Taylor 8 and 6, and C.H. Murphy 7 and 6. In the final, Travis held on for a two-up win over Stewart and in the process set new 9-hole and 18-hole records for the course. To triumph over a Scot was an admirable task to novice Americans.

In September, he beat Bayard Cutting Jr. in a Westbrook tournament and then tied for low score at Tuxedo. It was a successful season for the new enthusiast and he finished by winning handicap medals at both Oakland and Knollwood, though not faring as well in the match play that followed.

The Knollwood match play featured the start of a rivalry with Findlay Douglas that would last more than 21 years. Douglas—playing out of the Fairfield County Club and in many of the same events Travis would enter—was his nemesis in the early going, and in this first encounter he beat Travis by one up. Travis would not beat Douglas for three long years, but once he did he would never lose to him again in a national competition.

The press began to take notice of Travis during the Knollwood event and headlines read 'Travis a Surprise—Almost an Unknown Man.' One golf scribe wrote: "Mr. Travis has been doing some startlingly brilliant work on the links within a very short space of time. He has been playing the game but a little more than a year and was practically unknown to the fraternity of golfers until he tied a week ago at Meadow Brook for the handicap event and won the playoff last Friday. At that time, as well as yesterday, he made the lowest scratch score of the day, beating a small host of well known experts."

Others harped on his lack of competitive skill at other sports, calling him a mediocre billiard and tennis player and a cricket player as a lad, but one with no great proficiency. The reporter continued, "While he does not play a pretty game, he plays a very steady and cool headed one. When he gets into a bunker he wastes no strokes there. Furthermore he has nerve, which is an invaluable adjunct in golf."

Travis followed his fine play of 1897 with more successful events in early 1898. He posted an 81, the lowest round in the medal play at Lakewood, but then was eliminated in the match play semifinals. He equaled the amateur course record at Knollwood with a 77 and then won the cup with excellent match play rounds. He added a Dyker Meadow open tournament victory in June, and in July he lost in the finals of a Seabright tournament to J.A. Tyng, but posted another round of 77.

Travis in a rare jovial mood.

Entering the National Arena

B uoyed by his success, Travis entered his first national event in September of 1898, less than two years after his inaugural round of golf. For this to be possible for any golfer, much less for someone of Walter's age, was a remarkable accomplishment in its day—and it remains so a century later. It is, in fact, unprecedented in the history of the game in America. No one has even qualified for such a prestigious event with such sparse experience.

The fourth playing of the U.S. Amateur was held at the Morris County Golf Club in Morristown, New Jersey. A record 120 contestants were present, a total that had skyrocketed from the previous playing when only 58 players participated. Travis was content with his game and mentally ready for the challenge when he wrote: "About this time there grew up in me a desire to win the amateur championship." But another factor conspired against him.

"I had been overdoing it and a couple of weeks before the event I was taken down with malaria, from which, by the way, I have never fully recovered. A week in bed left me in poor shape and I had serious thought of not playing. I can recall as though it were yesterday," he wrote 23 years later, "an intimate friend urging me to have a shot at it on the ground that I was getting to be an old man and it would probably be my last chance. As I was only 37 I didn't feel that way about it and was quite sure my time would come sooner or later."

H.J. Whigham was the two-time defending champion, so the press was all abuzz when he failed to qualify for match play in the 1898 championship. The medal was captured by Joseph Choate, a young Harvard man playing from the Stockbridge Golf Club, but Travis advanced in a comfortable fashion. He plowed through his first three matches, beating J.I. Blair 4 and 3, J.G. Thorp 7 and 6, and Foxhall Keene 5 and 4. That brought him to the 36-hole semifinal against Findlay Douglas.

A rule change for the playing of the 1898 Amateur resulted in semifinal matches being extended from 18 to 36 holes. Had the previous standard been in effect, Travis might have claimed victory because he led Douglas by one hole after the morning encounter.

However, Travis's putter abandoned him in the afternoon round and Douglas soundly defeated him 8 and 6, prompting *Golf Magazine* to write about Travis: "Hitherto his attention has been principally directed toward getting on the green, the matter of getting into the hole having been lightly passed over. As a putter, he is lamentably weak in comparison with the rest of his game."

Others echoed this sentiment. One newspaper scribe wrote: "Time and time again he had a chance to either win or half a hole, and invariably he would let the opportunity slip through lack of confidence with his putter. Listening to every suggestion offered—all of which were pronounced infallible by those who championed them— and buying every conceivable weapon on the market—all of which claimed to be infallible—Travis has twisted and turned his body, struck more attitudes and handled more putters with a view to improve his weakness, than all the golfers in the country."

Travis knew the only way he would conquer the putting demons was to put the same attention to putting practice that he had to ball striking. Though he originally considered the pursuit trivial, he now realized that he was being beaten on the putting surfaces and this was enough to fire his desire to better his short game. He went back to the instructions of Willie Park, and took strength from Park's assertion that, "The man who can putt is a match for anyone."

During the 1899 season, Travis was focused once again. "The great value of putting was forced on my notice when I began to analyze my scores. The revelation was astounding! I found that in a score of say 76, and assuming one took on an average of two putts per green, totaling 36 strokes, this would be equivalent to nearly 50 percent of the score. In other words putting was practically half the game. So I set seriously to work to find out the fundamental principles of putting. Little of value was to be found at that time in books. This was in 1899. Accordingly the only avenue was in practice."

Before he could practice in earnest, however, Travis needed the right implement and the right technique for his style. Not unlike some Tour players today, he tried every model he could get his hands on. He tried wooden putters, gunmetal putters, straight-faced putters, cylindrical putters, mallet-headed putters, putting cleeks, cleeks, left-handed putting cleeks—"in short," he lamented, "the whole family of every conceivable kind of weapon that human ingenuity has evolved for the purpose."

This advertisement in the June, 1899 *Golf Magazine* convinced some that Travis should be considered a professional.

He also employed every setup that had ever been dreamed up—and 100 years ago there were some radical dreams rampant. "I have tried them all in every imaginable position—off the left leg, standing square, off the right leg, facing the hole; have had them equipped with long and short shafts with straight faces, with varying degrees of loft and, antithetically, with the face turned in—and, at times, have putted extraordinarily well with each and every member of the tribe."

To improve his stroke, he again went to every quarter for help. "I have tried putting with cut, with a follow through, with a chip, with a tap; with the hands taken well away from the ball before striking it, and the reverse; with light grip, with firm grip, with the left hand only, and again the right gripping firmly—all with varying degrees of success."

When he still failed to roll the ball into the hole with a high degree of success, he concluded: "The sum of it all is, that my experience shows conclusively that the really good putter is largely born, not made, and is inherently endowed with a good eye and a tactile delicacy of grip which are denied the ordinary run of mortals."

Still, Travis felt that if he kept at it long enough he could fashion a change that would propel him forward, especially in light of his conclusion in an article for *Outing* in July 1900, in which he stated, "Putting is largely mental, and on this account becomes so difficult.

Confidence is a prerequisite to good putting. Some players possess this quality in a greater degree than others—and accordingly are better putters."

Travis verbalized the lore that had infiltrated the game in the 1890s and is still employed today. Putts rattle into the back of the cup when they are meaningless—when the hole has already been won or lost. When the player strains and grinds, he can miss the shortest of tests; but when he slaps without stress, the ball often finds the hole effortlessly. He cited his daughter's wisdom when she asked, "Why is it papa, that when you have two for the hole you always go out in one, and when you have one for the hole you always take two?"

Despite espousing "born putters" and the need for confidence above technique, Travis haunted the practice putting green at Oakland and later Garden City for a great deal of 1899. He called putting an acquired habit, "a habit acquired by practice—like writing, only harder, and yet at the same time easier, paradoxical as it may sound. Easier, in that a neophyte at golf may, offhandedly, at the very first attempt, hole a putt of three to four feet with the greatest unconcern in the world, the while a good putter would be viewing the line from the ball to the hole, and vice versa, brushing away real or imagined worm casts, according to temperament, and finally settling down to the business in hand and ending up with an ignominious miss. Let it be remembered, in his favor, that back of him is the painful recollection of scores, hundreds, perhaps thousands, of similar putts that failed to drop."

He developed his own unique style and favored weapon, but he believed in understanding other techniques. "If you have only one line of attack, one weapon at your disposal, and find it ineffectual at any given time, the probabilities are that your work will get worse instead of better. It is a singular thing, apparently inexplicable unless on the theory that one's vibratory nerves are never exactly the same from day to day, that no matter how sound and well proven one's style may be, there are days when putts simply will not drop. I have found this so many a time. Do I keep on the same old groove? No, I have recourse to one of my alternate methods—and the change is usually beneficial."

The 1899 season created a legend about Travis that would follow him the rest of his career. He became known as one of the best putters of all time, and his confidence soared as he built upon a record of success with the blade. It was less his technique that propelled him—he used a short-shafted putter, gripped it well down the shaft, employed his palms in direct opposition to each other to produce a pendulum stroke with his body held motionless—than his desire. Travis willed the ball into the cup, and believed that every putt should find the bottom of the hole, regardless of length.

Travis had his share of success during the 1899 campaign, but early in the year his appearances were few. He won a 3 and 2 victory over R.C. Watson at Lakewood and had an easy time of it in an event at the Marine and Field Club. Then, although he played below his usual standards, he won the Oakland club championship for a third consecutive year.

There was also the embarrassing defeat of the Canadian team in an amateur international meeting where the United States team—comprised of Findlay Douglas, C.B. Macdonald, J.G. Thorp, Travis, and others—won every single match contested triumphing 47 points to zero. And there was the disappointment of losing to H.M. Harriman in the inaugural Metropolitan Open held at the newly opened Garden City Golf Club. Travis had been hit with a golf ball before his contest with Harriman and his right hand was badly swollen, inhibiting both his grip and his swing.

Largely through the efforts of Charles Blair Macdonald (winner of the first U.S. Amateur in 1895), the 1899 U.S. Amateur had been awarded to the Onwentsia Club in the Chicago area. Many of the New York-based players threatened to stay away, and as late as June 18, *The New York Times* reported, "Not many Eastern golfers will go unless they expect to land somewhere near the top. Tyng and Travis, two of America's ablest native players, are going to show in a practical way their disapproval of giving the championship to Chicago a second time in two years by remaining at home. The presence of both would assuredly add materially to the golfing excellence of the tournament, for each has recently been playing as fine golf as ever in his life. Travis perhaps a shade better than ever before."

Both men changed their mind as the tournament grew near, and while Travis was a more confident putter for the 1899 playing of the Amateur than he ever had been before, the results of his journey to Chicago were basically the same as they had been in New Jersey. He

Travis in his favorite red coat in 1899.

finished three strokes higher than John Reid's medal score win of
170, then plowed through the early rounds of match play. He dispensed with A.H. Smith 10 and 9, C.P. Lineaweaver 3 and 1, and the
medalist two up with one to play. Meanwhile, Douglas had dominated his opponents—winning two of his 36-hole matches with 11
holes left to contest.

They met on a sunny day and the crowds were out in force to
watch the matches. Unlike the championship in New Jersey the previous year, Onwentsia had gone all out to attract patrons and entertain them with on-course amenities and gala events every day. "A
vaudeville show each night is our motto," said club member H.C.

W. J. Travis,   C. B. Macdonald,   Findlay S. Douglas,
Bronze Medallist.   Bronze Medallist.   Champion, 1895.   Runner-up, '97 and '99.   H. M. Harriman,
                                   Best Preliminary Score, '97 and '99.   Champion, 1898.   National Champion, 1899

THE SEMI-FINALISTS OF 1899.

The U.S. Amateur semi-finalists in 1899. (L to R) Travis, Charles
Blair Macdonald, Findlay Douglas, and H.M. Harriman.

Chatfield-Taylor, and sure enough the mood was festive as the players battled in the semifinals.

In the morning match, Travis was outdriven on every hole except one by Douglas. The latter's iron play was also quite commanding. Around the greens, both players squandered shots and many holes were won with scores of bogey or higher. Travis took the fourth hole to go one up, but Douglas countered by tying the match again on the fifth. The talented Harvard competitor J.G. Thorp served as caddie for Travis, and he made an error on the sixth hole by declaring a ball Travis had hit out-of-bounds, when in fact it wasn't. The extra stroke that Travis was assessed sealed his fate on the hole, and as quickly as he'd been one up, two holes later he was one down. The only other hole of the morning that Travis would take was the 15th. By morning's end, Douglas was four up.

Travis fought back in the afternoon, starting with a victory at the first. After 27 holes, he was only one down. Douglas, however, took command of the game on the back nine and soon was dormie five, though Travis still refused to fold. He won three straight, the win on the 16th coming when Douglas missed a putt that a reporter said he could have kicked in. When they tied the 17th the match was over, and Douglas once again advanced to the final.

Travis had played better than the previous year but had still fallen short. He knew it was unlikely he would outdrive his opponent in the future, so his thoughts turned to an improvement in his short game as his only route to a more successful outcome. To this, he would dedicate himself in the future.

The final year of the 1800s also was the beginning of yet another facet of Travis's remarkable career—golf course architecture. In August, Travis was approached by James Taylor, a member of the Dyker Meadow Club, about a piece of property in Vermont that he was interested in building a golf course on.

The First Foray into a Future Career

Travis journeyed north with Taylor and John Duncan Dunn, a son of legendary Scottish greenkeeper Tom Dunn, who had come to America in 1894. Travis had met Dunn in his role as professional at Ardsley-on-Hudson Country Club in New York and the two felt their talents were complementary.

Travis was enamored of Vermont from the moment he entered the state and glowed about the possibilities that the tract of land offered. Both Travis and Dunn felt a world-class course could be installed on the rolling fields framed by the gentle nearby mountains of the Taconic Range. Natural green sites were in evidence, a few groves of trees could be utilized, and a small brook trickled through the property. The architects advised Taylor to move forward with his plans and he did so posthaste.

By late August, Taylor had secured the property. By Labor Day, enough subscribers had committed to proceed with the golf course, and just days later a crew of 42 workers arrived with teams of horses, drag pans, a six-ton steam roller and a will to work. Travis and Dunn worked the site for tees and greens—designing in the field as they went—until the routing was set. The course was to be more than 6,000 yards long, at a time when few in the country surpassed 5,500. Natural contours were to be enhanced by dozens of carefully constructed bunkers. Greens of all shapes and sizes were added. In an era when many course planners were content to march off 100 yards to the next cross bunker and merely leave stakes to designate greens, Travis and Dunn sought to establish a layout with carefully considered features that would take a principal position in American golf.

Dunn returned to New York shortly after the initial routing. Travis, though, spent a good portion of September and October supervising the crew, adding hazards, seeding greens, playing test shots, making adjustments to the way holes were situated, and enjoying the hospitality at the Equinox Hotel during a mild autumn in northern New England.

Work continued until the 23rd of November and Travis expected the course to open the following June. The quick taste of golf course

36

architecture was pleasing to the hardware executive who had just taken up the game three years previously. He planned to dabble some more as time allowed, and he also planned to return to Vermont.

As a result of his involvement at Ekwanok, Travis played less competitive golf in the closing months of the 1899 season than he had previously. He had been beaten in the finals of the Shinnecock tournament in July by A.L. Ripley of Massachusetts, but bounced back with wins at Nassau and Scranton in October. His loss in match play at Lakewood in the Thanksgiving Day tournament was attributed to bad driving—a sign of his commitment to dedicate himself to the improvement of his putting and his design responsibilities that had curtailed practice.

In January of 1900, *Outing* carried the following note: "Yet another anomaly was made apparent in the defeat of W.J. Travis, whose perseverance and brilliance for two years have made his name a synonym for success. Covered with trophies won on a hundred fields against the best players of the two years, he must, we think, notwithstanding his eclipse at Lakewood, be placed high on the roll of honor, and no player ever worked harder for or more deserved the niche which he has attained."

As Taylor had initiated at Ekwanok, another group of gentlemen on Long Island sought to establish a world-class course in their neighborhood. Bankers, lawyers, architects, judges, and industrialists were joined by another newly empowered golf course architect—Devereux Emmet—to establish the Garden City Golf Club. Though Travis was not a founding member, he was convinced to join during the seminal year and from that day forward—and continuing today in the Travis Room and through the Travis Memorial Tournament—Garden City has been synonymous with Walter Travis.

As he settled into his routine at Garden City he installed and utilized a practice technique for which he was given inventive credit, though its origin may have preceded him. As Grantland Rice noted in a 1927 *The American Golfer* article, "He devised the scheme of smaller holes on the practice course at Garden City, holes only a trifle larger than the ball. He practiced here for hours and when you can drop them steadily in a two-inch cup, one double the size looks like a keg."

Although Travis is credited for this form of practice, Horace Hutchinson claimed that he was the victim of a Mr. Macfie, who

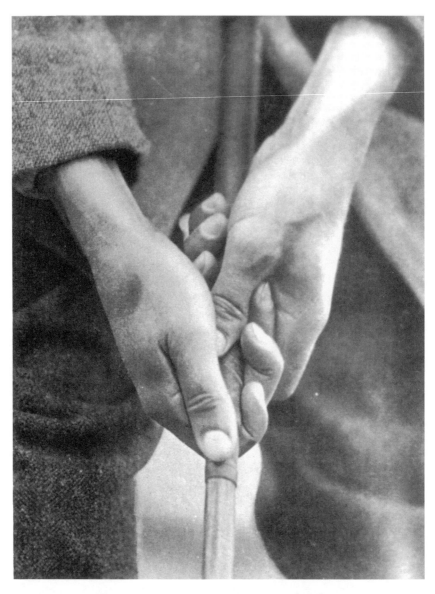

The putting grip that led to unparalleled putting success
(Courtesy of *The Art of Putting*).

developed a similar practice regimen as early as 1885. After he had eliminated Hutchinson from a championship by the lopsided score of 10 and 8, Hutchinson said Macfie "entertained me for the rest of the way by telling me how he did it, namely, by practicing putting at tiny little holes, like egg-cups, in his garden. When he came to the comparatively big holes on the links they looked so receptive that it seemed impossible to keep his ball out of them."

Spending his time perfecting his putting, Travis developed a visual aid that remained at his putting core for the next quarter century. "One of his main angles in regard to putting," Rice wrote, "was to imagine you were driving a tack into the back of the ball and let the putting blade go on through. He considered putting largely a right-handed affair and the right hand predominated in his grip. The left was merely a steadying aid."

Travis would also force himself to obey a regimen that could be time-consuming. He would drop four balls on the green, each three feet away from the cup on each point of the compass. If he sunk all four, he would move the balls six inches farther away and try again. He kept moving them back until he was 10 feet away. If he missed, Travis would return to his original position and try again until every ball found the bottom of the cup.

Despite his dedication to improvement, it is doubtful that even the confident and talented Travis could have suspected what riches were about to be won as the year rolled over to 1900.

National Champion

Travis closed out 1899 as a major figure in American golf, but no one had any idea how much further his star would rise in the several years that followed. From a coterie of only those intimately involved in metropolitan New York area golf, he would soon become the number one competitor in the annals of American tournament play, and his exploits would be watched by nearly everyone in the game.

In the early months of 1900, Travis could be found on the practice putting green at Garden City whenever his schedule and the weather allowed. Content with the techniques he had perfected for driving and iron play, Travis sought a style and routine that suited him for the ground game. Though some would tire of this work, Travis loved to practice and could spend hours at a time focused on the task at hand. When the first handicap list of the New York Metropolitan Golf Association was published in the new year, Travis knew his work had been properly rewarded—he was listed as one of only three scratch players in the section—along with Findlay Douglas and H.M. Harriman.

Early in 1900, Travis moved his family from Flushing to a small house not much more than a block from the Garden City Golf Club. His daughter was nine and his son was six, and Bartlett remembered that the reason for the move was "on account of the golf." In an August 1952 article for *Metropolitan Golfer,* Bartlett recalled those early days at Garden City: "I associated my father with a glistening red and black bicycle. After we moved to Garden City, there was still the bicycle, with my daddy on it, but gradually something new was added. There appeared a golf bag, slung over his shoulder. I can see the combination to this day disappearing down the hill by our house. He would come home in the late afternoon, don a pair of knickers and then he, the bicycle and the golf bag would roll down the hill and ride off into the mysterious beyond. As I grew and became more curious the mystery was gradually revealed. It seemed that my dad was always going to or arriving from the golf course, which was only down the hill and up another, about a block from our home."

Bartlett slowly came to realize that everything about his father revolved around golf. The walls of the house were covered with golfing prints, the bookcases filled with golf books, and every available surface covered with trophies and cups. Shelves had to be added to absorb the overflow. In the attic, Travis set up a club making and repair shop, bolting a vice to a steamer trunk and assembling the heads, shafts, leather grips, whipping, and pots of glue needed to customize his weaponry. Before long the shop consumed the entire top floor.

Travis's research didn't end there. "Later he started experimenting with different grass seeds," Bartlett recalled. "Our front lawn resembled a botanical crazy quilt in spots where he planted various blends of seeds." There was no escaping the fact that Walter Travis was a golf fiend.

In April he opened the competitive season at the Atlantic City Country Club, winning the 36-hole qualifying round and eventually defeating Findlay Douglas for the first time in match play. Travis won the final by four up with two to play, and the victory was secured with crack putting, prompting *Golf* magazine to write about his newfound putting skills, "Mr. Travis goes at golf in just the same way he used to tackle cycling...in the same systematic manner he has thrown himself heart and soul into every phase of the game of golf. There is no closer student of the ancient history of the sport than the new captain of the Garden City Golf Club."

Later in April, Travis had the opportunity to judge himself against a true representative of the royal and ancient game, and the best player in the world at the time—Harry Vardon. Vardon had landed in the United States earlier in the month, played one match in the north and headed to the warmer climates of Florida, where he dispensed with every team that he faced. Returning to the Northeast, Vardon was invited to play at Oakland against the better ball of Travis and James Douglas, the host professional. The match was played on April 25, 1900, in front of a sizable crowd.

"I know we got the worst of it," Travis commented later, "but I do not recall by what margin." The tally was six up with five to play in the 36-hole match and Vardon shot 77-79 on his own ball, though the memory most were left with was the length of his booming drives. "Vardon at that time was playing with wooden clubs with quite small heads of dogwood, with leather faces and rather limber shafts," wrote Travis. "Some of his shots were a revelation to most of us in respect of distance." Although Travis made some pars, he was not on his

Harry Vardon demonstrates his putting technique while Travis watches prior to their exhibition match at Oakdale in 1900.

best game, while his partner was "wildly erratic" according to *The New York Times.*

On May 5, Travis was part of a New York team that played the best Philadelphia area golfers at the Philadelphia Country Club for amateur bragging rights in the Northeast. He beat H.M. Forrest 5 up with 4 to play in a lopsided 49 to 7 hole drubbing by the New York-

Vardon prepares to drive while his better-ball opponents,
James Douglas (left) and Travis observe his technique.

ers. Both these tune-ups were but a prelude to the second Metropolitan Championship scheduled for May 23–26 at the Nassau Country Club in Glen Cove.

Although the golfing centers of Boston, Philadelphia, and Chicago were not represented (along with the wealth of talented players in the universities), pundits felt that the next U.S. Amateur champion was among the ranks of the 54 players who teed it up at the Met. In the qualifying rounds, Travis and Douglas were paired together and their golfing styles were in sharp contrast—though the results were nearly identical. As 'Oldcastle' wrote in the July issue of *Golf:* "Travis drove off the left leg, his right foot being an inch or so back of his left. Douglas, on the other hand, played in what is regarded as the orthodox way—that is, the style adopted by the great majority of golfers, with his right foot advanced two or three inches in front of his left. With his irons, again, Douglas shows great power, but perhaps not more so than Travis, though each man seems to get the carry on the ball in a different way. Douglas does everything with his arms, throwing them out after the ball, and getting in all his work with them. Travis, on the contrary, depends to a very large extent on his wrists, and, like Vardon, he lays into the ball at the last moment with great effect."

This contrast in styles reflected the open, looped St. Andrews-type swing that Douglas brought with him when he came to America, and the new American style that Travis had developed in his own study of golf. With his power, Douglas hit the big fade, watching shots drift right when they went bad. Travis had mastered the compact inside-out motion that kept the ball low and also turned it over—producing overspin and run—which moved the ball slightly right to left as it scooted along the ground for the few extra yards that Travis needed to compensate for his lack of power. This first year of the 1900s marked a pivotal moment in the evolution of American golfing skills. Travis was about to supplant Douglas as the dominator of the amateur golfing scene, and his swing would usher in a new era of technique as well.

The two never met in the final because Allan Kennaday of Montclair beat Douglas two-up in the quarterfinals, and then Kennaday himself was ousted by Harriman. Travis and Harriman squared off in the final on a windy and rainy afternoon, one in which Travis remained focused on the job at hand despite the distractions. His victory prompted *Golf* to write, "Throughout the tournament he played a consistent game, not brilliant one day and second rate the next, but always high class; and of such players are champions made. From being the best medal-player in the country, Mr. Travis has made himself a match-player of the highest rank, and no doubt further honors await him."

Travis did not have to wait long to fulfill that prediction. In June, his final tune-up for the amateur championship came at Oakland and his game was as sharp as it had ever been. On a course he knew well, Travis posted a 76 to win the qualifying medal before easily dispensing with every man he faced, including an 8 and 6 drubbing of W.G. Bamwell in the final.

By this time, more and more, Travis was being asked to write accounts of his play and of golf in the metropolitan area. Despite an active competitive schedule, his design responsibilities at Ekwanok, a business life, and his young family, Travis accepted the invitations and wrote of his adventures. As his personal letters had demonstrated, he had a flair for the language and enjoyed the outlet.

Although Travis was known for smoking a cigar during matches, he occasionally enjoyed his pipe instead.

For the July 1900 issue of *Outing*, the newly crowned Metropolitan champion and Garden City member previewed the upcoming U.S. Amateur championship at his home club. "Garden City is one of the few clubs in the country which can lay claim to possessing links," Travis wrote, "in contradistinction to the scores and scores of golf courses; and those who took part in the Metropolitan Championship on these links a little over a year ago will find a material change in the distances of the holes, particularly on the outward journey. The lengthening of the first, third, fourth, fifth, seventh and eighth holes cannot but be considered a very great improvement."

Though founding member Devereux Emmet had designed the links at Garden City, Travis had been coerced into assuming the role of chair of the green committee upon his induction as a member. The two men started as dear friends and golfing companions. Over time, though, that would change as they fussed with the course they both loved. Travis found fault with the layout from the start, and although it would be nearly a decade before he put his stamp on the bunkers and greens, there was acrimony growing in Garden City.

The course had been extended nearly 400 yards to 6,070 yards for the championship. Travis wrote: "The alterations in length which have been made now call for one, two or three good shots to reach the green, as the case may be, there being practically no opportunity for the player foozling a stroke to make it up on the next and be on a par with the man who has played each shot cleanly. Garden City, as it is now, is no place for the pawky player, and furnishes a splendid test of first-class golf."

Travis lamented the fact that the field may have grown to as many as 150 players and that the normal round of two and a half hours could well stretch to three, especially when "there are not more than thirty or forty players in the country who may fairly be regarded as standing any chance of reaching the third round."

His worry was not borne out, as only 121 entries were received, in large part because the western contingent from the Chicago area decided to stay at home. Nevertheless, it was the biggest amateur field yet, with 57 different golf clubs represented. After knocking in a three-foot putt—the result of nearly holing his tee ball on the final hole—Travis posted an 81 in the afternoon round of qualifying. When matched with his morning 85, it produced a medal-winning score of 166.

Golf magazine made the following note of Travis and the resolve he showed during the week. "It was apparent from the outset that Travis had made up his mind to win, and he left no stone unturned to secure his success. He had his plan of campaign marked out as carefully as though it had been a piece of military strategy. He had previously figured out for himself the play best suited to his game for every single hole, and he kept steadily to that plan of action, but with scant regard to what his opponent might be doing. He kept himself as free as possible from every kind of annoyance and distraction; the deliberation with which he walked and played was the index to his mental attitude. He did not become excited or nervous at a crisis for the simple reason that he decided that he would not. Perhaps he took a leaf here from the mental scientists; at any rate, he was enabled to hold his own against all the depressing and depleting influences consequent upon a six days' contest of brawn and nerve in the worst of weather. And finally he played with his head, and used his brains, the latter ingredient being conspicuously absent in the work of some of his competitors."

The course had been baked by weeks of hot, dry weather and officials wondered about the choice of dates forwarded by the USGA—suggesting a reversion to the fall time slot in subsequent years. Despite the heat, more than 500 spectators followed the important matches and retired to the well-appointed clubhouse when the action slowed.

After a 2 and 1 scare in the first round against Robert Watson, Travis raced through his opponents, winning 8 and 7 from James Stillman, 6 and 5 from Charles Hitchcock, and 11 and 10 in the semis against A.G. Lockwood. Findlay Douglas did about the same, setting the stage for another great duel between the two titans. Though an *Outing* article after the tournament portrayed Travis as a rock, by his own admission that is not the complete story. "There is no undue deliberation in his work on the links," wrote The Sportsman in his View-Point column, "and literally no nervousness. In truth, he appears in all his matches to be the least concerned of anyone on the course."

Upon reflection, Travis contradicted this. "For the first seven or eight years I was always nervous in competition, strung up to such a pitch that I was painfully conscious of my heart beating away like a drum...but I contrived to keep my nerves at least partly under control."

By now, both men knew their opponent's game by heart. Douglas was known for his mediocre game around the greens, and until that season, Travis had not demonstrated substantially more talent. Douglas could drive the ball 225 to 240 yards—a considerable wallop for the time. But until 1900, Travis rarely surpassed 170 yards off the tee. On the dry fairways of the course he knew so well, however, for the 1900 Amateur, Travis was reaching the 200-yard mark.

In the morning round Douglas won the long holes, but Travis more than compensated with short-hole victories, and excellent imagination around the greens. "Eight times Travis got into the sand hazards or in the long grass," the article in *Golf* reported, "and each time with his iron he laid himself dead for the hole. Such consistent work surmounting difficulties surely cannot be called luck. It is good play, play of the highest order, in which the brain carefully reasons how defeat may be averted, and the hand trained by long and arduous practice successfully executes the cleverly conceived plan of action." Travis led three up after the morning round.

In the afternoon the game was about the same, with Travis holding a two- or three-hole advantage throughout the match. On the fourth hole, Douglas had a chance to get back to only one down but missed a putt of 15 inches. What made the final two hours quite memorable for the contestants and the hundreds of spectators that were following the match was the weather.

The first hint of real trouble came as the players played the seventh hole. The wind that had been gently blowing most of the day began to swirl and rage, while inky black clouds advanced on Garden City. As the players reached the ninth tee, the fury broke loose and torrents of rain fell while the wind howled. "The small tent erected there for the refreshment purposes was never more acceptable than when nearly the entire gallery crowded in like sardines in a box to escape a drenching," said *The New York Times*. "As it was, fully a score of men were soaked to the skin and half a dozen ladies met a similar fate."

Back at the clubhouse things were even worse. A gigantic tent of more than 150 feet in length where diners were enjoying lunch "collapsed like a crushed opera hat beneath a furious gale of wind. The wind blowing under the canvas made a sound not unlike a miniature tornado." Several people crawled out of the wreckage with minor injuries, and the press and caddie tents were leveled as well.

After a very brief delay in play and the passing of the storm cell, Douglas rallied once more. He won the 10th hole with a birdie three. When he also captured the 15th, he was only one down. It was there that the rain began again, and the gallery deserted the players as they slogged onward. At the 16th, Travis was the beneficiary of a rub of the green over which no one had control. Unable to reach the long hole in two pokes, Travis played a short third that reporters characterized as wretched. But the wind carried the ball over the bunker that it would have otherwise been deposited in, and dropped it within a few feet of the flagstick. The same wind had grabbed Douglas's second shot and brought it 400 yards from the tee and into the fronting bunker. After Douglas had difficulty escaping the bunker, Travis made his putt and won the hole.

At the 17th, it was raining so hard that the pinches of sand used to tee the golf ball were washing away before the ball could be hit. The gloom also prevented anyone from seeing where a long shot landed. Travis topped his drive while Douglas stroked his best of the day—a 250-yard boomer down the middle. Douglas made birdie while Travis struggled for bogey. Travis was now dormie one.

It is best to let *Golf* describe what happened on the par-3 18th—the final hole of the championship: "The home green was now a lake, several inches of water completely covering it, and both tee balls landed with a splash. The play on the green at the last hole will not soon be forgotten by those few who saw it. Devereux Emmet, the vice-president of the Garden City Club, stood near the hole with a broom trying to sweep the water away, and having the same success as Mrs. Partington had with the Atlantic Ocean. The water grew deeper every minute, but the game had to be finished. Putting was out of the question, for the ball would not roll an inch. Playing the odd, Douglas did not loft with sufficient strength, going only halfway to the hole, while Travis, making a perfect shot under the circumstances, laid his ball dead with a flop in six inches of water, and so won the amateur championship of America by two up."

It may have been a finish unlike any other. But just three years and nine months from his first swing with a golf club, Walter Travis had captured the most prized possession in American golf. It had culminated in a grueling week. Most of the matches had been played in 90-degree heat and like most of the players, Travis had lost several pounds. Despite the circumstances, the new champion had played

Walter J. Travis at Garden City Golf Club during his first
U.S. Amateur victory in 1900.

eight complete rounds with an average score of slightly over 81 strokes—exactly bogey for the course. His rounds had included one outward half of 35 and one inward half of 38—both course records.

As the press glowed about his win, Travis headed to Vermont to celebrate with a round at Ekwanok where 18 holes were now open. The Ekwanok Board of Directors voted Travis an honorary membership as raves about the course he designed were matched only by the accolades over his triumph. Spirits flowed freely at the Equinox Hotel.

By July 24, Travis was back in tournament form for the Shinnecock Open. He tied for low qualifying score with club member A.M. Brown but won the 36-hole playoff for the medal. He romped through the matches, finishing with a 12 and 11 crushing of Roderick Terry to capture the President's Cup. In the process, he set a new standard at Shinnecock by going around in 74 strokes and 150 for a continuous 36-hole loop. He also paired with Dev Emmet for a second-place finish in the foursomes.

Travis was back at Ekwanok in August, playing an exhibition match to formally christen the course. He was partnered with fellow amateur Charles Blair Macdonald against host pro George Low and Newport (RI) Golf Club professional W.H. Davis. The close match ended with a one-stroke victory for the professionals, and more pronouncements that Ekwanok was one of the finest courses in the country.

Travis was quietly seeking additional design work, though it was hard to pursue given his other responsibilities. He did bring John Duncan Dunn with him on one of his visits to the Essex County Golf Club in Manchester-by-the-Sea, Massachusetts, and the two of them suggested alterations to the 1893 layout. Travis was a regular visitor to Essex, and over the course of the next several years he would remodel a few of the holes. Unfortunately, when Donald Ross took up residence at Essex he eventually obliterated all of the Travis work and put his own stamp on the layout.

It turned out that Travis had two more victories in him before the season closed. At the Tuxedo Club in August, he once again pulled the hat trick—winning the qualifying, gaining the Tuxedo Cup for victory in the match play, and setting a new course record with a 71. At Westchester in November, he won the qualifying but was defeated in the matches by W.L. Thompson of Baltusrol. He bounced

The eighth green at Ekwanok Country Club—Travis' first course
design—shortly after opening in 1900.

back at Lakewood in a December event, taking the Lakewood Cup
by once again besting Douglas in the final.

It had been an astounding year: eight victories, numerous course
records, many qualifying medals, the respect of his golfing peers,
and the accolades of the sporting public.

Practical Writing about Golf

During the winter that followed his breakthrough year, Travis was contacted by *Golf* magazine to share his golfing wisdom with the public. Already an accomplished writer, and now with a Cinderella story to tell at a time when Americans were listening, Travis was a natural to reveal his secrets of rapid golfing ascendancy and to recount his competitive successes. His extensive articles began to appear early in 1901. Not long after, Harper Brothers approached him with the possibility of compiling the writings into a full-length book.

Practical Golf first appeared in June of 1901—approximately the fifteenth golf book published in America—and it was head and shoulders above the other North American efforts. Patterned after Park's *Game of Golf* that Travis had devoured when learning the game, the book went far beyond the instruction the earlier one offered. Chapters on clubs, balls, caddies, handicapping, the rules, course construction and upkeep were ground-breaking, and the book established Travis as both a competent writer and an American authority on all facets of the game. *The New York Times* published a positive review on June 14, 1901, stating, "It is a great comfort to find that a player so eminent stands solidly by the ancient principles. To those who have watched his career closely the reasons for his success are sufficiently apparent, and they are of the kind which we always like to hold up before our boys as sure to lead to success in any calling or enterprise. Disraeli once told the young men of the University of Glasgow that the way to success is to try, to fail, and to analyze your failures. This has been Mr. Travis' method in golf."

The competitive fires, the taxing writing deadlines, and business pressures took a toll on Travis in the first few months of 1901. He was exhausted, depleted, and in need of some rest. His doctor prescribed an extended trip with some relaxation and perhaps some recreational golf.

At the behest of John Reid and the entire tournament committee, it was decided to move the U.S. Amateur from its Fourth of July playing date in 1900 to a fall date for 1901. Oppressive heat had drained the players and had kept the onlookers to a minimum. The

This formal portrait served as the frontispiece in Travis' first book,
Practical Golf, published in 1901.

wise decision allowed Travis plenty of time to prepare for a defense
of his title at the Country Club of Atlantic City in New Jersey, September 9–14.

Before going abroad, Travis entered the third Metropolitan Amateur Championship as the defender. His heart wasn't in the matches

Putting during his successful defense of the U.S. Amateur title at the Atlantic City Country Club in 1901.

at Apawamis and by his own admission, "the best I could do was to get as far as the semifinal, when I got licked by Charlie Seeley at the first extra hole after a tie." Seeley was smothered by Douglas in the final, 11 up with 10 to play.

Travis was already in transit to Scotland when the June 1901 issue of *Outing* raised an issue that would haunt Travis for a number of years. At the time, the rules governing amateur play and the status of amateur competitors were still under development. Some felt that amateurs must remain 100% clear of any financial arrangements remotely related to sports of any nature in order to maintain amateur status. This included revenue of any nature, endorsements in any quarter, and gratuities bestowed in any endeavor. Others felt that a law more akin to the rules that govern amateur play today was in order. A battle was being waged in the press, and, unbeknownst to Travis aboard the steamer, he was the subject of one skirmish.

The incident that prompted the attack took place on a trip to Florida during the previous spring. Travis had traveled with J.C. Powers, Arthur Lockwood, and the editor of *Golf,* Van Tassell Sutphen, to visit John Duncan Dunn, the manager of the Florida Golf Association. While there, the four lodged at the Tampa Bay Hotel. Editor Caspar Whitney, the author of the *Sportman's Viewpoint,* called the issue of semiprofessionalism an "evil which as present menaces the game most seriously." He continued: "Herewith I challenge the right of entry to all amateur golf tournaments of Walter Travis, New York, who won the amateur championship of America at Garden City, L.I., last July, and of A.G. Lockwood who reached the semifinals of that tournament. The conduct of Messrs. Travis and Lockwood in receiving free hotel board and railroad transportation this spring, during a Florida golfing campaign, makes them obviously ineligible to rank as amateurs. By the rules of every amateur game, including golf, they are professionals, for if they did not receive money for their services as touring hotel billboards, they did receive its equivalent in several hundred dollars worth of board and lodging and railroad fare."

Many came to the defense of Travis in his absence. Dunn wrote, "Travis was four days in Florida on the West Coast, at Belleair and Tampa, but he did not play in a single competition, although tournaments were going on at nearly every links and he was urged to play by his friends stopping at the different resorts, all of whom wanted him to join their parties. He did not go to Florida as the guest of the Plant system, or of any hotel. The visit came about in this way: Morton Plant is up for membership at Garden City and is one of Travis's friends. Belleair is his hobby and he is proud of showing off the place to his friends as any millionaire is to show his country home. He invited Travis to go down on his private car for a visit. The party broke up after two days at Belleair, and Travis went on to Tampa Bay, starting back for New York at the end of the week."

When the *Outing* article was reprinted in *The New York Sun,* several readers were outraged, including C.S. Cox who wrote, "People who are really conversant with the facts about amateurism in sports know perfectly well that golf is the cleanest and most absolutely free from professionalism of any sport played and so far ahead of the same sport in regards to amateur standing of its members in the old country that any comparison would be ridiculous. Caspar Whitney, when he first commenced trying to purify amateur sports in the colleges, wrote fearlessly and to the point, and too much credit cannot be given to him for the stand he took; but, like all small-minded men, he has arrived at a point where he imagines he is arbiter of all the sports in the country, whether he knows anything about them or not. In this particular sport of golf we all know his practical experience is absolutely nil."

R.H. Robertson, president of the USGA, also responded to the *Sun* coverage, indicating the organization's willingness to investigate any impropriety, but seeing none in this accusation and admonishing Whitney to bring future protests to the secretary of the USGA—not air them in the pages of the magazine. Though Travis never needed to respond to the charges, the issue would be back in subsequent years.

Research in the British Isles

Despite his doctor's warning, Travis bypassed the suggested rest and was joined by Charles Tappin and E.W. Jewett on an extended golfing junket. From mid-July through mid-August they played 36 holes a day, including multiple rounds at Troon, Prestwick, St. Nicholas, St. Andrews, Elie, Carnoustie, North Berwick, Muirfield, Edinburgh Burgess, Hoylake, Formby, West Lancashire, Mid-Surry, Woking, Sandwich, and Deal. "It was a liberal education," Travis later wrote. "Those which more particularly appealed to me were Prestwick, Formby, and Sandwich...the latter destined some three years subsequently to figure rather conspicuously on my second golfing trip."

The purpose of this trip was threefold: much-needed relaxation, a testing of talent against some of the stronger players from Great Britain and a symposium on the design features of the venerable Scottish courses. The trip opened Travis's eyes and he came away with a new respect for golf in the British Isles.

"In this country it is difficult, if not impossible, for the average American player to realize and properly appreciate the existent conditions of play on the other side, as exemplified by their leading links, there being such a radical difference in their physical configuration in relation to our courses. It is doubtful whether any verbal or written description can adequately convey any accurate idea of the beauties of the simon-pure links which abound on the other side of the pond. We really have nothing like them. These links are not the growth of a few years; rather they are the product of centuries."

Travis was taken by the sand hillocks of all shapes and sizes that framed the links. He was amazed by the presence of four or five bunkers (American courses would only have one), awed by the thin-bladed, velvet-silky grass indigenous to the links land and the sandy soil that supported it, and impressed by the British budgets that allowed upkeep of their courses for a fraction of what Americans were spending for inferior playing fields.

"Golf, with us, is mostly of a kindergarten order. The holes are too easy, and there is too much of a family resemblance all through. Our courses seem to be laid out not with reference to first class play, but rather to suit the game of the average player. Really good links develop really good players, a few remarkably so, while the general standard of play is at the same time very sensibly improved."

Travis railed against American green committees who stifled appropriate bunkering of holes for fear it would irritate less talented members and pined for the undulating character of the terrain that yielded natural holes of high order. He realized how the ground dictated the vagaries of good shotmaking and the difference in style of play exhibited by the talented British golfers. He understood how greens that flowed seamlessly from fairways encouraged the bump and run, whereas American "push-up" greens required a lofted pitch.

He found it peculiar that players didn't know the distances of the holes, but rather played by feel, able to craft shots of varying distances with the same club in different situations. He found links without precise demarcations at the tee box and therefore considered the visitor to be at a distinct disadvantage to the local player, especially when the folds of the earth introduced deception into the puzzle.

He was impressed by the caddies, who, despite not knowing the exact distances, knew how to club a player shortly after taking his clubs. This was in addition to the services that they provided in teeing the ball and in following its flight—even when it headed for impenetrable rough. He was also amazed by the standard of play. "Were a team of twelve of our best men to go over, it is pretty safe to say that every man would be beaten on our side."

Finally, Travis was pleased by the pace-of-play, at a time when an 18-hole round in this country was always played in less than three hours. "All of their strokes are played with more dash and decision than are general with us. Moreover there is no time wasted over strokes through the green; a glance of a second or so as to direction, about the same time for the address, and the ball is off. Their best players seem to recognize that the business in hand is to hit the ball, and that it is futile to endeavor to spend some time in an effort to mesmerize it."

Travis was welcomed cordially by the most sophisticated and accomplished Brits, and games were arranged at every stop. At Barnton, he posted a 75 against Angus Macdonald; on the North Berwick links, he bested Norman Hunter; and at St. Andrews, he toured the Old Course with 80-year-old Tom Morris who fashioned

Travis playing the Old Course at St. Andrews with
Old Tom Morris in 1901.

an 88 in their play. Observed Travis: "His short game, especially his running-up approaches, was very good and served to give a faint idea of the grand game that characterized his earlier years."

Many of the prominent golfers of the day took note of the U.S. Amateur champion's visit. He was greeted with the respect and conviviality that was appropriate to a golfer of his stature. Several encouraged him to stay on and play at the British Amateur scheduled for Muirfield. But Travis was under doctor's orders to relax, not to grind over another championship.

"Be it remembered that Mr. Travis comes to this country to recruit his health, having been run down, and that if he obeyed his doctor he should not be playing golf at all," wrote The Scotsman, whose column was carried by many of the local papers.

He continued: "Beginning at Troon and Prestwick, Mr. Travis gave a good account of himself against some of the western cracks. According to Ben Sayers, and all who saw him play, he is a complete master of the game. Our first word is one of warning to our Scottish amateur cracks just to keep their eye on America. It has been the fashion hitherto rather to hold American golfers cheap, and to think that ages will elapse before they can challenge with any success our home performers. To judge from Mr. Travis this is quite a mistake. Mr. Travis' visit has not been quite a case of *veni, vidi, vici*, but his performances have convinced all who have seen them that native-born American golf has a future to be reckoned with and to be held in respect." Prophetic words, indeed.

Harold Hilton also took notice of Travis and contributed several paragraphs on him to his weekly *Sporting Chronicles*. "In style the American champion is essentially what may be termed a made golfer, for his is a style which by the wildest stretch of imagination could not be called ornate. Still it boasts useful attributes; it is business-like and determined, and is one in which no energy is wasted."

Hilton praised Travis's driving style, noting he was beyond the average and had "mastered the art of scientific hooking. But sound as his driving is, I think the charm of the American's game lies in his iron play. With a quick switch of the wrist he drives a really long ball with either a cleek or an iron, and, what is more, it is a long ball invariably straight, while with his pitching mashie he is exceptionally sound, seldom making a mistake."

Travis and Hilton enjoyed a round together at Hoylake, the first time the reigning British and American champions had met in a match of any kind, with Hilton prevailing five up with four to play. One of Travis's favorite outings was at Richmond, playing with J.H. Taylor in a foursome with Fry and Worthington—two leading English players. Little could anyone of them imagine the repercussions that would result from Travis's next visit to the United Kingdom.

Defending with the Haskell

Back in the States by August 20, Travis began his practice routine in preparation for the defense of his amateur crown, once again concentrating on putting into the undersized cups on the Garden City practice green. Travis was interested in the new Haskell ball that had recently been patented in Akron, Ohio. The ball was the result of experimentation and dumb luck. While waiting for a friend to join him for a round of golf, Coburn Haskell was fiddling with a basketful of scraped elastic bands, wrapping them into a small ball. Every once in a while the ball would escape from his grasp and start bounding around the room, displaying a much livelier reaction than the gutta percha balls that Haskell was about to play with in his golf match. When his golf partner, who worked at the Goodyear plant, was finally ready to go, Haskell turned to him and said, "If you would cover this ball with gutta percha for me, I believe I could win some golf matches with it." His partner, Bertram Work, did just that. When the ball was hit by a professional for the first time, it cleared a bunker off the first tee that even the longest of drives with a gutty had barely rolled into. Some refining of the surface of the sphere helped to give it lift and keep it on flight, and a star was quickly born.

Travis dabbled with predecessors of the Haskell ball, but kept his involvement under wraps until shortly before the tournament at Atlantic City. Players who tried the ball knew it added length with the longer clubs, but believed that it was difficult to control around the greens. Shots that were gained elsewhere were frequently squandered on the carpets. Travis, however, had developed a feel for this type of ball with practice and was not afraid to debut it at the championship.

"I was keen to experiment, although many friends tried to dissuade me," he wrote later in *The American Golfer*. "I contrived to get hold of two of the new creations, and on the day before the qualifying round thoroughly tried them out. I found that against the wind the guttie about held its own, that it was more reliable on the short approach and in putting, due doubtless to one's greater familiarity with it, but, on the whole, the newcomer had a slight edge in its favor. Its chief point of advantage over the old ball lay in its greater carry, especially off irons, and, with the wind, in its greater run. These features, however, were not without drawbacks at the time, as allowances had to be made for the liveliness, especially in putting, and one could hardly expect to accommodate one's game in a single day to the change."

Guided by the maxim, "Be not the first by whom new is tried, nor yet the last to throw old aside," Travis cast his fate to the Haskell, despite the admonishment of many of his close friends and biggest fans. It was a bold move for the defending champion, but one that proved visionary.

Travis dismissed J.E. Porter 5 and 3, C.B. Macdonald 7 and 6, and P.H. Jennings 2 and 1, before running into his old nemesis, Findlay Douglas in the semifinals. *The Times* called the match "a magnificent fight between the two masters of the game, followed by a large throng of spectators." Travis fell behind early, but by the conclusion of the morning round he held a two-hole lead. Douglas battled back in the afternoon, squared the match after 27 and then took the lead with a par on the 10th. Travis countered with a win on the 11th and then began a string of draws until the 16th, where Travis went one up. Douglas was not to be denied and amid intense excitement he snared the 17th, bringing the match to the home hole dead even. A tie there sent the match into two extra holes and Travis finally prevailed.

Walter Egan, a young Chicagoan on the way up, had cruised through the other half of the field and stood ready to test the 40-year-old Travis. Egan was a Harvard student and cousin of Chandler Egan who would win his first U.S. Amateur three years later. The two boys had learned the game by building a course through their neighbors' yards and down the avenues of town in 1896. Unfortunately, the match was postponed for a week when President William McKinley was assassinated. Due to work and school commitments, the final could not be rescheduled until the following Saturday.

Crowds were slim for the match on a cloudy and cool day. Egan played with poise and skill and finished the morning even with the defending champion. A large gallery gathered for the afternoon round and watched in astonishment as Egan fought back from the two-hole deficit that he created for himself with errant drives.

Travis clearly was not on his game, but still managed to move ahead on the eighth hole and never looked back. The match con-

Travis at the conclusion of the 1900 campaign—the year
he broke through into the national spotlight.

cluded on the 14th; Travis had successfully defended his coveted
crown. Though the win confirmed Travis's position at the top of the
golf world, it had far greater ramifications. The gutty ball was dead—
competitors who played the wound ball had hit it farther and scored
lower—and the golfing public wanted them.

American manufacturers jumped on the bandwagon. Goodrich produced the first model, quickly followed by the Kempshall Company, then Spalding and Worthington. British ball makers balked, in large part due to Harry Vardon's gutty ball that he marketed so heavily. By 1902, the transition was in full swing in America, but the walls were just starting to come down in Britain. Eventually, golfing clubs would be redesigned to create greater loft when the ball was struck and courses would be lengthened to protect par. Travis's bold move had not only prompted a change in golf balls but a change in golf as well.

Travis kept a low profile for the rest of the year. He won again at Westbrook in October—capturing both the qualifying medal and the trophy for winning the match play—but that was his last major tournament of the year. At about this time, Travis left the hardware company that he had been associated with for 15 years and joined an advertising agency. He could foresee a time when he would not have room for any pursuit outside the world of golf. Through his course design, writing, and tournament play, Travis was now one of the best-known sports figures in the country.

Late in 1902, Travis offered design suggestions to a group at the Flushing Athletic Club who were playing a short and primitive layout plotted by Tom Bendelow along Whitestone Avenue. As golf slowly took over as the dominant outdoor activity, some members broke away to form the Flushing Country Club. The nine-hole course was improved through Travis's suggestions, and an additional nine holes were eventually planned by Dev Emmet. In 1923, the Club changed its name to The Old Country Club. The organization survived until 1936, when it fell victim to the Depression, and the land was sold to developers.

The Old Man

Perhaps it was the match with Walter Egan for the 1901 Amateur championship, or perhaps just the turning of one more year of the calendar, but by 1902, the first referral to Travis as "The Old Man" appeared in the media. Travis had turned 40 in January of 1902 and many of his battles were against younger and younger players. In fact, he was often *twice* as old as his competitors. However, it would still take more than age to knock the champion from his pedestal.

As Genevieve Hecker, a New Yorker who was winning all the comparable women's events of the day wrote in her 1902 book, *Golf for Women:* "We have failed to produce feminine players whose game has been a refutation of the tradition that it is necessary to begin young. It is true that there is no such encouraging example to the portly matrons and elderly maids in the ranks of their own sex as the men have in our present Amateur national champion, Mr. Walter J. Travis. It is said by many good judges that he has reached the limit of his play, and that he cannot improve further, but this was said of him in 1899, when he disproved it most conclusively by his wonderful string of victories and the increased length of his long game in 1900."

Travis did scale back his playing schedule in the new year, concentrating on the major events, but still entering a number of club events throughout the metropolitan regions. *The New York Times* noted that "he has a record of having won more club tournaments in his career than any other player," and few could refute it.

However, disagreement remained about another issue. The matter of amateur versus professional once again surfaced in 1902. Joseph E.G. Ryan wrote an article entitled "Is Walter J. Travis an Amateur?" in *Golfers Magazine.* His contention stemmed from a letter that Travis wrote on May 7, 1900 to a clubmaker—and Ryan reproduced it in the magazine for all to see. It read in part: "Young John Reid showed me at Philadelphia the wooden clubs you made for him. They certainly are beauties. If you feel disposed to send me, without charge, a couple of drivers and a brassy, I shall take pleasure in using them, and hope that by doing so you may get orders from other players." Travis went on to specify the exact details of what weights of club would be best for him and pleaded for them to be sent as quickly as possible.

Ryan went on to detail other charges stemming from the Florida hotel incident and the whitewashing that the USGA had given similar incidents. He asked questions about the products Travis's name was associated with. "Why did Travis boom the Henley ball? Why did he recommend the socket screwhead driver? Why does he advocate the aluminum club? Why is Mr. Travis' name subscribed to testimonials for 'gripites,' liniments, and other paraphernalia supposedly of benefit to golfers?" He concluded, "When an 'amateur' champion deliberately offers to tout for a clubmaker the writer thinks it is high time to acquaint genuine amateurs with the 'plugging' methods of the individual who is supposed to be the ne plus ultra of the American amateur golfing world."

Travis made no direct response to this charge, feeling he had said enough about it a year earlier when he'd been asked if he had anything to say about the Florida charges. "Certainly not: nothing at all," was his only response then, and he stuck by it. The nagging issue would eventually contribute to Travis's decision to scale back his competitive schedule—but that would not come for another decade.

He did allude to the USGA's problem with the definition of amateur status in a widely-read commentary entitled "Golf Outlook for 1902" in the April 26th issue of *Collier's*. Travis had been an early proponent of a match between the best amateur golfers of Great Britain and America, but knew the opposing team would need financial contributions to be able to visit the States. Such monies would deem them professionals in some eyes. "Already there is some talk of arranging for the visit of a team of British amateur golfers this year, a consummation devoutly to be wished. But for the somewhat strained, not to say quixotic, definition of an amateur by the present administration of the United States Golf Association, there is no doubt that an international team match would before this have been definitely arranged. As it is however, this ruling of the USGA may possibly bar the way toward any such meeting."

Travis went on to offer his opinion about the choice of date for the amateur championship, the increase in regional championships, how to rid greens of worms and worm casts and what's wrong with

Travis offered putting tips in a series of instruction
articles for *Golf Illustrated*.

the game. Travis felt the game suffered from faddists—"the man
who plays, not from any pure innate love of the game, but simply
because it is considered the correct thing and happens to be the
fashion. They are the ones who are chiefly responsible for elaborate
club-houses, involving a heavy drain on the finances of the clubs,
and various transitory side-shows, which do not legitimately belong
to the game but which are embarked in with the vain hope of retain-
ing their capricious interest." Tolerance was not Walter J's strong
suit, though the purists agreed with him wholeheartedly.

Travis's first big event of 1902 was the Metropolitan championship, played at the Tuxedo Golf Club on May 28. He won the single
round of qualifying with a 76, four strokes better than second-place
finisher Charles Blair Macdonald.

Due to an unusual draw, Travis faced his nemesis Douglas Findlay
early in the contest. And while it was clear that both players were
sharp, Travis was at the pinnacle of his game. Despite going out in
a two-over-par 38, Douglas found himself four down to Travis at
the turn. Three holes later, Douglas was out of the championship.

FIG. 13

PLAYING A HANGING LIE

Playing a hanging lie in deep grass with suit, cigar, and derby.

Fig. 28

PUTTING GRIP

The putting grip.

Travis was encouraged to keep playing because the course record was at stake, but he lost his concentration on the first post-match hole and took a seven. He still finished with a sterling 72. Travis remained untouchable through the four days of competition, besting F.A. Marsellus in the 36-hole final 11 up with 10 to play.

The U.S. Amateur was played at the Glen View Club in early July, visiting the Chicago area for the fourth time in eight years. Once again, Travis was the medalist with a 79. Travis plowed through his first two matches and was three up on young Chicagoan Eben Byers after the first nine holes of their 18-hole quarterfinal match. But suddenly the mood and the match changed on the inward trek. "Although I played well," said Travis, "my opponent played a little better, especially on the second nine, where he ran down long putts

FIG. 25
PUTTING OFF THE LEFT
LEG

FIG. 26
PUTTING OFF THE RIGHT
LEG

FIG. 27
STANDING SQUARE

Seen any U.S. Amateur champions putting like this today?

FIG. 22
ADDRESS FOR A BAD LIE

FIG. 23
TOP OF STROKE

FIG. 24
FINISH OF STROKE

Does this look like the swing of a champion?

on the 10th, 12th and 13th greens, respectively, squaring the match, and, by virtue of a fine four at the 16th got in front for the first time, and stayed there. Byers is an exceedingly skillful player, and he has lots of nerve. The score he made was too good. There was nothing but good golf all the way, and the young man deserves his victory."

Spalding Golf Guide editor Tom Bendelow called it one of the best matches, amateur or professional, ever played—postulating that had it been scheduled for 36-holes as previous tournaments, Travis may have fought back for the win. But, he noted, "John Reid, Jr., who caddied for [Byers], preceded Byers as a golf champion at Yale, and it was Reid's steadiness yesterday that doubtless had much to do with Byer's uniformly good game. He and Reid were at times cool as cucumbers. Travis, on the other hand, began to get nervous on the incoming journey. This was not appreciably noticeable in his game, for he made a 39, but it probably made him tremble a bit to see the young man coming after him so much in earnest." Byers was convincing in two more matches during the championship, but, on a rain soaked course, fell in the final 4 and 2 to unheralded Louis N. James.

Travis had hoped to hold the title three straight years, a hallmark in the era that signified dominance, and usually resulted in the retirement of the trophy in the winner's hands. He was disappointed in the outcome, but took it in stride and promised to dedicate himself to regaining the title.

That summer was noteworthy in the life of eight-year-old Bartlett Travis as well. Every summer, Bartlett and his sister Adelaide took a long vacation with their mother visiting their aunt in Canada. Bartlett looked forward to the trip in large part because his aunt had two automobiles—a Pierce Arrow and a Winton—and Bartlett was car crazy at this age.

Once school was out for the summer, Bartlett was allowed to join his father at the golf course while Travis practiced. The boy would chip and putt, but had yet to take the game seriously. One day near vacation-time Travis asked his son if he would like to become a top golfer, to which Bartlett responded in the affirmative. "Well, you stay down here with me this summer and I will make a golfer out of you," said his father. "We can come up here in the afternoon and I will really show you how. I think you are ready."

Bartlett was stunned, and hesitated to agree since he loved the vacation so much. To the elder Travis it was a statement that was absolute and irreversible. Bartlett later wrote: "Nothing more was said about my staying home and at the end of June we left for Canada. After my return there were no more invitations to join him in the afternoons. I missed them, but my father was intolerant of any lack of enthusiasm where golf was concerned and I am afraid he thought I had let him down. Sometimes I feel that those days when we practiced together were as close as I ever got to him."

Low Amateur

Travis had never played in a U.S. Open, but since the 1902 championship was scheduled for his home course it seemed that this was the perfect year to do so. No amateur had yet captured the trophy, or really contended in the seven playings of the event.

Travis was on edge during the opening day, playing in front of a home town crowd with the guys who got paid for playing. "Somehow I could not manage to get going and 82 for each round was anything but meritorious," he wrote. Laurence Auchterlonie, the visiting Scottish pro, was in the lead with 156.

Travis was also the subject of a high-stakes wager that must have upset his balance. "Some time before the meeting a well-known amateur had made a heavy wager that I would beat any two professionals. These were selected as Stewart Gardner and Willie Smith. I knew of the bet, and was much chagrined at my poor showing the first day. So the next day I 'girded up my loins' and made up my mind that I would give of my best. At the home hole I was told I had to get a three to tie with Gardner, who had finished second to Auchterlonie. Willie Smith, with whom I played, I had already beaten. I had left myself with an uncomfortably long putt, which I knew had to be holed. I can conjure up the scene again—the waiting crowd surrounding the green...my own feelings, and likewise those of the man who had the temerity to back up his belief in my game. He was in the gallery, on tenderhooks I felt sure, being a bundle of nerves.

"All these thoughts flashed through my mind in the brief space of a few seconds, the while I was stooping over to address the ball. It is extraordinary, perfectly marvelous, the multitudinous thoughts that can flit through one's mind with lightning-like rapidity in a crisis. But when I settled down to the business in hand, the crowd, all outside reflections, faded into nothingness, and I was keenly intent on only one thing, the holing of that putt. It went down!"

Travis finished tied for second—the highest finish by an amateur to that date, and a mark that would remain the standard for 11 years—until Francis Ouimet stunned Vardon and Ray in 1913. Travis also posted a tie for the lowest round of the tournament, a 74, with the champion Auchterlonie, and bested him on the second day with rounds of 74 and 75 to Auchterlonie's 74 and 77. His first foray into the professional's world had been a success, and Travis planned to try his luck in the Open again.

Travis spent part of the spring revising his book, *Practical Golf.* The book had sold out the first printing within one year, so a second edition was published in the summer of 1902. In the preface Travis wrote, "With the ink scarce yet dry it becomes necessary to issue a second edition, and I frankly own that I gratefully appreciate the ready recognition which the first met with. Growing out of more extended observation and experience, a new chapter has been added on Hazards; also new chapters concerning the development of the Haskell ball and the introduction of aluminum clubs."

Travis noted the craze for aluminum clubs and admitted to using a few during the 1902 season, especially a niblick "of fearful and wonderful design, something like a bludgeon...only more so. It was the most unlikely looking weapon to accomplish the purpose for which it was created, having a large sole, slightly rounded, but it did the business effectively. All through the season I had one of these weird things in my set, as well as a cleek and a midiron."

He thought the benefit of the aluminum clubs was the ease with which a player could precisely locate the center of gravity due to the homogeneous nature of the metal compared to wood. He especially liked the aluminum putters and employed them for several seasons. "No long apprenticeship has to be served, as in the case with the wooden putter—and also to some extent with all iron clubs—to ascertain the particular point with which the ball should be struck to cause it to run straight." Travis also pointed out that aluminum doesn't rust or require cleaning.

In the winter of 1902–1903, Travis spent considerable time and effort to see that a visit of British amateurs would occur in 1903. Despite the fact that Travis had been beaten by many of the same players while visiting the United Kingdom in 1901, he felt that the best American players had improved in the two seasons since, and that they could at least give the visitors a good game. A tour was set for late summer and early fall.

Bolstered by a winter of putting practice, Travis swept the early season events in the metropolitan region. He won the qualifying medals and the match play contests at Lakewood, Atlantic City, and

Garden City as he prepared for the Metropolitan championship on May 27, 1903.

In light of his early season play, his failure to advance beyond the first round at the Deal Golf Club was shocking. Travis blamed his performance on an incident that took place during qualifying. When the scores were posted, it appeared that Dr. D.L. Culver of Jersey City was the medalist with 166, and Travis was second with 168. However, it was suggested that several of the posted scores in Culver's total were inaccurate and the matter was brought before the MGA executive committee, of which Travis was a member. Being a contestant, Travis excused himself from the deliberations, but when all was said and done, Culver was disqualified.

Travis claimed he lost his composure as a result of the proceedings. He was ousted by John M. Ward when he lost the final hole of the match. It was his earliest exit ever from the tournament.

Travis rebounded by capturing the invitational at Knollwood Country Club, beating F.H. Hoyt, the reigning Maine state champion by 11 up with 10 to play. Travis posted an amazing string of subpar rounds to win the cup—71, 67, 68, and 72—the 67 slashing the previous course record of 71 by four shots, and being recognized as the first sub-70 score ever made in competition on any Metropolitan-area course. He noted a comparison to the first time he had entered a handicap event at Knollwood—merely five years previous—when he posted 84 and 83.

Bolstered by his performance in the 1902 U.S. Open, Travis entered the 1903 edition at the Baltusrol Golf Club in Springfield, New Jersey on June 26. He was clearly off his game, and unable to post a round in the 70s. He finished tied for fifteenth, 19 strokes off Willie Anderson's winning score of 307.

A Third Major

As the 1903 U.S. Amateur at Nassau Country Club grew near, there was controversy regarding the way a champion would be crowned. Englishman G. Herbert Windeler, president of the USGA, strongly favored no qualifying and all matches decided over 18 holes, with the exception of the 36-hole final. Travis opposed the idea and offered this opinion: "I thoroughly believe in the retention of the preliminary round. No man should be considered a finished golfer, certainly not a champion, unless he can combine reasonable proficiency at score play with high abilities as a match player. Moreover, it is essentially an American idea, and a very good one, and its abandonment now would be a tacit admission that we have seen the error of our ways, which I, for one, am not prepared to admit at all."

Travis's plea fell on deaf ears, and for the first time there was no qualifying, with 140 entrants squaring off in matches right out of the starting gate. Defending champion Louis James was beaten immediately and Jerome Travers—a new sensation playing in his first national event, and competing at his home club—fell in the second round. So did Findlay Douglas, and Travis cited this as further proof that the all match-play format was faulty.

Travis breezed through his matches, including a confrontation with future golf course architect A.W. Tillinghast who was playing out of the Philadelphia Cricket Club. The final—against Eben Byers, the man who had knocked him out in 1902—gave Travis a chance to avenge his loss the previous year. "Both played brilliant golf, the best, in fact, of the tournament," reported the *New York Sun*, "but Travis always held the upper hand, and seemed to have the match safe at all times. He played with his usual machine-like regularity, and was cool and unruffled throughout. Travis' game was almost faultless. In the morning he established a new competitive record of 73, which, while not equaling his 72 a week ago, nevertheless stands as the record from the fact that the other score was made in practice only."

The match was very poorly attended. In fact, it was the smallest crowd ever to witness a final. In large part, this was due to the weather. Black clouds had been accompanied by thunder and nearby lightning for much of the day. Seconds after Travis closed out Byers on the 14th green, the heavens opened. Many in attendance were soaked by the time they reached the clubhouse, a half-mile distant.

In capturing his third national title, Travis had accomplished a goal he set five years previously. "I am satisfied with winning three championship tournaments," Travis told Joseph Marsten for an article in *Munsey's Magazine*. "I had set my heart on doing that. Whether I ever win another I do not care. I shall not retire; I love the game too much. I do not know whether I shall appear in next year's contest. That is looking too far ahead; but I shall not retire." Perhaps the golfing gods heard Travis say that he didn't care if he won another, because, despite medalist honors four more times, he would never visit the winner's circle again in the U.S. Amateur.

The conclusion of the amateur coincided with the visit of the Oxford and Cambridge Golfing Society of Great Britain to the region, part of their five-week tour of this country's finest facilities. All along their path, the top collegiate golfers and champion club golfers were lined up for matches.

The schedule that developed consisted of a dozen events played against an intercollegiate team, as well as teams from Massachusetts, the Western Golf Association, Chicago Golf Club, Shinnecock Hills, the Metropolitan Region, an All-Eastern team, an All-U.S. team, and teams from New Jersey and Philadelphia. The Brits visited the finest courses America had to offer: Myopia Country Club, Essex Country Club, Chicago Golf Club, Glenview Golf Club, Garden City, Nassau Country Club, Baltusrol, and the Philadelphia Country Club. The grand finale of the tour would be a Match Play Tournament for selected amateurs and an Open event for professionals sanctioned by the USGA at Ekwanok on September 14–17. Travis was part of three matches, including the Metropolitan team, the Ekwanok squad and the All-U.S. team.

The British side began with 11 players: Captain John L. Low, Norman F. Hunter, Charles Hugh Alison (a future golf course architect), G.D. Barne, H.W. Beveridge, J.A.T. Bramston, C.N. Day, H.G.B. Ellis, T. Mansie Hunter, P.W.H. Leatheart, and D.F. Ranson. Unfortunately, the travel and accommodations wore on the visitors and only seven players made it to the end of the tour at Manchester, Vermont.

At Nassau, Travis paired off against the team captain: "I won my match against John L. Low, beating him at his own game—approaching and putting. At the time I was using a center-shafted aluminum putter with a ball-and-socket arrangement in the head which permitted any kind of adjustable changes of both lie and lift. It worked very well." In fact, the point Travis secured was the deciding blow in a five to four victory over the Brits—the only time the team was beaten in the entire extravaganza.

The final at Ekwanok—where Travis felt like the host—was noteworthy. The site was a comely departure from the urban courses the team had visited, and it made a positive impression on H.W. Beveridge, who later wrote, "Those of us who made the hot and dirty journey found it well worthwhile, for Manchester was a lovely spot nestling between two ranges of magnificently wooded mountains and standing 3,000 feet above sea level. Whether or not it was the combination of rarefied air and a charming course, the golf was of a high standard."

The British team had prevailed in seven of the nine matches they had played, tied one, and suffered their only loss against the U.S. All-Star team at Nassau. Otherwise, they had dominated the competition on courses they were seeing for the first time. At Philadelphia, they won 11 matches to none against the best golfers in the Philadelphia region. At other sites, the results were similar.

The British may not have been impressed with the American game, but they were impressed with their treatment. Beveridge wrote, "Of one thing we were certain; in the matter of hospitality Americans were unbeatable. We were having a wonderful time."

With success on the links and gracious hospitality afterward, it was not surprising the visitors were amenable to continued international competition. After a Chicago match, Beveridge wrote, "At night there followed a great dinner, particularly interesting in that during the speeches the question of International Golf Matches between Britain and the U.S.A. was broached for the first time, so far as I know, and eventually resulted in the Walker Cup matches."

Four days at the Equinox was the social highlight of the five-week tour. Lavish dinners were accompanied by liberal libations, and the British contingent soaked it up. It drove one New York writer to postulate on their readiness for the tournament. "The unvarnished truth is that the Englishmen, with possibly two or three exceptions, were utterly fagged out and in no condition to enter a contest. Those cognizant with the facts know that the visitors have been wined and dined to an extent sufficient to upset the most stolid and phlegmatic of temperaments." Nevertheless, 32 players, including the seven visitors, teed up for the opening round of what *The New York Times* called "an important international contest."

On the second day, the premier match was played between Norman Hunter and Travis—Travis having defeated Hunter at Shinnecock Hills two weeks earlier in the Oxford and Cambridge match played there. *The Boston Herald* tagged the return encounter "the hardest contest ever witnessed on the local links. Both men were at the top of their game and displayed rare form." But this time Hunter was a 1-up winner, and the demise of the reigning U.S. Amateur champion left America's hopes for the individual championship pinned on the golfer he had defeated in the national finals just two weeks previously, Eben Byers.

The final between Hunter and Byers was set, but due to rain the match was postponed until the following day. Whether it was another night of excessive indulgence or just sheer exhaustion, the players did not bring their 'A' games to the match the following morning. *The Boston Herald* reported, "Both men were unsteady at times. They were especially ragged on the putting greens. Hunter lost the match on the 17th hole. He topped his tee shot and went into the brook. It took him three to reach the green and he holed out in five, while Byers laid his second shot dead to the hole and went down in three. The Britisher could only halve the last hole and lost by one down."

The news wires went wild with the outcome. *The Boston Herald* crowed, "Byer's victory in probably the grandest tournament ever held in this country stamps him as entitled to rank with Mr. Travis at the top of American golf. During the tournament, Byers disposed of four of the strong Oxford-Cambridge team in rapid succession, a performance at once remarkable and brilliant when the class of his opponents is considered."

The tour that Travis had desired so deeply had achieved many ends. It fueled the competitive fires of the new wave of American amateur golfers. It set in motion a series of matches that eventually would give birth to the Walker, Curtis, and Ryder Cups. It demonstrated to American observers the power and touch of players with years of golfing wisdom under their belts. And, it solidified Travis's place in the world order. He decided he needed to test that position further in 1904.

The 1904 British Amateur

Travis began 1904 with yet another competitive success. The Old Man had a few close friends in the world of golf: Robert Hunter who had migrated to the West Coast was one, Charles Blair Macdonald of Chicago was another, and Donald Ross of Pinehurst was still another. Ross had moved to Pinehurst in 1900, devoting himself to the courses there, and Travis was growing increasingly interested in this phase of golf. The first North and South Amateur Championship had been played at Pinehurst in 1901, but Travis had not attended. For the 1904 playing, Travis found himself at Pinehurst, which suited him in every way save one—Pinehurst was in a dry county and liquor had to be smuggled in. This problem gave rise to the Tin Whistles, a group of wily, determined men who, like Travis, were not to let golf get in the way of their drinking and smoking.

Despite their antics, or maybe because of it, Travis won the 1904 North and South by defeating Charles B. Corey of Boston. In the process, Travis set the course record of 69—the first time par had been broken on the 5,176-yard Number 1 course at Pinehurst.

Travis believed that the Pinehurst courses could be so much more than they were, given their sandy soil and gentle undulating land forms, similar to what Travis liked about British courses. He discussed the matter with James Tufts, but nothing was done during this visit. Travis, however, knew he would be back for another try.

As he weighed his options for the 1904 season, Travis gave consideration to a competitive trip across the Atlantic. He was a big fan of life in the United Kingdom. His mother and father had both been born there; he had honeymooned there in 1890 with Anne; he had spent considerable time around London as a young hardware merchant in 1895-1896; he had returned for a six-week golfing excursion with his pals in 1901; and he had hosted the Oxford and Cambridge Golf Society during their successful tour of the United States the previous fall. When Travis returned from his annual sojourn to Palm Beach in late winter, he announced his decision to go to Sandwich for the Amateur.

As the reigning United States Amateur champion, he had no reason to believe he would receive anything but a cordial welcome. In

Travis at Pinehurst where he advised on the design of the courses
and won the North and South four times.

THE ROYAL ST. GEORGE'S GOLF CLUB.

Amateur Golf Championship Tournament, 1904.

The Amateur Golf Championship Tournament, open to all Amateur Golfers, Members of any Golf Club, will commence at Sandwich, on TUESDAY, 31st May—under this reservation that, in the event of the number of entries being such as to prevent the final heat being started on the morning of Friday, 3rd June, the Tournament may commence on Monday, 30th May—when the Trophy, value £100, and four Medals, will be competed for under the following conditions:

1. An Amateur Golfer is a Golfer who has never made for sale golf clubs, balls or any other article connected with the game; who has never carried clubs for hire after attaining the age of 15 years, and who has not carried clubs for hire at any time within six years of the date on which the competition begins; who has never received any consideration for playing in a match, or for giving lessons in the game; and who, for a period of five years prior to 1st September, 1886, has never received a money prize in any open competition.

2. Competitors shall enter for the competition through the Secretaries of their respective Clubs, who, in sending in the names, shall be held to certify that the players are *bona fide* Amateur Golfers in terms of the foregoing definition.

3. The Entrance Fee shall be One Guinea, and must be received by the Secretary of The Royal St. George's Golf Club, not later than Wednesday, 25th May.

4. The competition shall be played by holes, in accordance with the Rules of the Royal and Ancient Golf Club, and the Local Rules of The Royal St. George's Golf Club.

5. The draw shall take place on Thursday, 26th May, and shall be conducted as follows:— Depending on the number of entries, such number of byes shall be first drawn, as shall, after the completion of the first round, leave 4, 8, 16, 32, or 64 players, and one draw shall decide the order of play throughout the competition,—those who have drawn byes being placed at the head of the list of winners of the first round, and taking their place in the second round in the order in which their names then stand.

6. Each game shall consist of one round of 18 holes, except that the final heat shall consist of a match of 36 holes, and shall be played on a separate day.

7. In the event of a tie in any round, competitors shall continue to play on until one or the other shall have gained a hole, when the match shall be considered won.

8. The winner of the competition shall be the Champion Amateur Golfer for the year and the Trophy shall be held for that year by the Club from which the winner shall have entered. The winner shall receive a gold medal, the second a silver medal, and each loser in the semi-final round a bronze medal.

9. All entries shall be subject to the approval of the Committee of The Royal St. George's Golf Club.

10. All disputes shall be settled by the Committee of The Royal St. George's Golf Club, whose decision shall be final.

FRIDAY, 27TH MAY—THE ST. GEORGE'S CUP.
Open to all Amateur Golfers.

For the Best Scratch Aggregate Score of Two Rounds.

The winner will receive a Cup, value Twenty Guineas, as a Memento. Entry Money, 10 6.

A Meeting of Delegates will be held in the Club House, on Wednesday, June 1st, at Five o'clock p.m.

Competitors and Secretaries of Golf Clubs will be admitted to the Club House and Green as Visitors without payment, from Wednesday, May 25th, until Saturday, June 4th, both days inclusive.

By order of the Committee of The Royal St. George's Golf Club,

W. RYDER RICHARDSON,

Secretary.

. The Railway Companies will issue First and Third Class Return Tickets to Sandwich, Deal or Ramsgate, on surrender of a Certificate which can be obtained from the Secretaries of The Royal and Ancient Golf Club of St. Andrews, The Honourable Company of Edinburgh Golfers, The Prestwick Golf Club, The Royal Liverpool Golf Club, The Royal St. George's Golf Club. These tickets will be available from 21st May to 13th June, both days inclusive.

THE CLUB HOUSE,
SANDWICH,
April, 1904.

Broadside announcing the 1904 British Amateur at Royal St. George's Golf Club.

fact, many of the British players he had met in 1901 had encouraged him to stay over for their championship. Many members of the visiting amateur team in 1903 had also suggested that a visit by Travis in the future would be appreciated. In addition, the Sandwich golf course had been one of Travis's favorites on his previous trip. He declared so on numerous occasions, writing, "Taken all in all, Sandwich is a very fine course—much better than anything we have." He had been unusually complimentary about all the British links, and after his 1901 trip had stated that American golf course architecture had a long way to go before it approached what was available in the old country.

Travis was further encouraged through a letter that he received. His friend and fellow Garden City Golf Club member, Devereax Emmet, spent part of each year in England training dogs and scouting golf design features for Charles Blair Macdonald. On March 23, 1904, he wrote a long letter to Travis, which began, "My dear Walter," and read in part: "I hear you are coming over to Sandwich to have a try at the Amateur Championship. I hope this is true. I will be there to root for you. I have been riding hard all winter and have only played golf twice, but have gone out in a field and driven a ball quite often. I am going to be a month at Portmarnock in Ireland before I go over to Sandwich. Let me know where you will be staying at Sandwich, and when you go there."

Emmet continued with these prophetic words: "If the weather is calm I think you will win the thing, but if it is very windy the chances are in favor of some powerful slogger like Hunter or Maxwell. The carries are terrible against a stiff wind. I wish the links were Prestwick. They don't begin to know how good you are over here, which will be greatly in your favour." In a postscript he added, "Get over as early as possible. That links wants a lot of knowing. As I remember it the greens are not large, and most of them must be approached from short distance with a mashie or iron, not a putter."

Anne looked forward to the trip as well. With her mother now living next door in Garden City and domestic help on board at home, she felt she could leave 13-year-old Adelaide and 10-year-old Bartlett. Walter expected first-class treatment throughout and the vacation would do her some good.

There were others at the Garden City Golf Club who shared Travis's enthusiasm for the effort and wanted to lend their support.

"Judge Horace Russell, president of the club as well as president of the Metropolitan Golf Association, organized a little party to escort him overseas and to lend to him moral support," wrote H.B. Martin. "On the board of strategy, besides Judge Russell, were the well-known after dinner speaker, Simeon Ford, James Taylor, fellow club members and Edward Phillips, a friend of Travis's from the Apawamis Golf Club. Travis had such a wonderful reception in 1901 that he told his friends that the British would be even more cordial this time since he had accepted their invitation to have a 'go' at their championship."

From the moment the party set foot on English soil in early May, it was apparent this was not exactly going to be the case. Few, if any, of the champion amateur golfers would play practice matches with him, and at some locales the invaders were shunned. To make matters worse, Travis had fallen into one of the worst slumps of his career, and when he was observed by interested Brits they came away laughing at his chances in the tournament.

The visiting foursome started at St. Andrews, and both there and at the next stop in North Berwick, Travis was terrible. As desperate players do, he bought a new set of clubs at the second stop, hoping for salvation, but realized little change. He found a sympathizer in Ben Sayers, who suggested a regime of training that Sayers had found success with—a total abstinence of smoking and drinking. Travis had tried that once early in his career—but concluded it made a mess of his game, especially on the putting green—and decided that he would never let golf get in the way of his cigars and whiskey again. "I told Benny of my experience, much to his horror and surprise. His system of training, it appeared, not only tabooed all indulgences of this sort, but also embraced massage treatment—rubbing in Elliman's embrocation all over. In return for his kindly interest I compromised on the rubbing, and to cement the bargain he loaned me his favorite spoon. I don't know that the perfunctorily-performed massage treatment had any real virtues, but I do know that the spoon was of valuable assistance. Many a time since, Benny, have my grateful thoughts wafted over to you at North Berwick, and also to Taylor, Harry Vardon, and Braid for the keen and sympathetic interest taken in my welfare that week."

It is obvious from this statement that the professionals were the ones who welcomed Travis in the U.K., while the amateurs feared him and treated him in a less than friendly manner. J.H. Taylor had arrived at Sandwich a week before the Open to watch the Amateur, and in his book *Golf: My Life's Work,* he singled out the spoon Sayers had given Travis as a critical element in his victory. "Mr. Travis was not too proficient with his iron clubs, relying on his spoon, which he used with remarkable effect and precision when faced with a long shot up to the green." Taylor had met Travis in the United States in 1900, and even though the match they intended to play at Garden City had been rained out, Travis had gone out of his way to sit with Taylor and swap golfing stories. They then teamed up for a four-ball when Travis was visiting Mid-Surrey in 1901. Wrote Taylor, "so when I met him again at Sandwich I felt I was welcoming an old friend."

Travis delayed his arrival at the Royal St. George's Golf Club in Sandwich, not wishing to influence his impression of the course with substandard play. When the party did arrive in town they were told that due to an oversight, no quarters had been reserved for them at the Royal St. George's Hotel where all the golfers were staying and they would have to make other arrangements at the Bell Hotel. It was even harder for officials to explain that a locker had not been set aside for Travis and that he would have to change his clothes in a public hallway and store his clubs in the professional's shop. At first incredulous, then angry, Travis did not hit it off with tournament officials. He turned down their invitation for dinner, which the English viewed as a direct insult. Both sides thought the other impolite and unfriendly right from the start, and as Travis wrote, "For the most part we had to flock together, inside and outside, and not a finger was lifted nor a single step taken by a soul to make us escape the uncomfortable feeling that we were pariahs."

Judge Russell suffered further indignation when he was asked to pay a sovereign just to enter the clubhouse—this after extending many personal courtesies to the Oxford and Cambridge players nine months before. The Judge had not only lodged three players from the visiting team at his house on Long Island, but had paid their entry fee to view the annual yacht race and other events. At one function the Judge asked if any team members were present and the only response was a perfunctory wave of the hand by one player. There were other members of the team on hand for the championship "but not a single thing was done by any one of them at any time in return for his many gentle courtesies. And the same remarks apply with equal force in the case of Mr. James L. Taylor, who did so much for the visiting team at Manchester, Vermont," Martin wrote. "If he should ever go across he should look them up, so two or three said as they presented their cards, and they would try and do their best to reciprocate. Mr. Taylor's cards on arrival on the other side were never acknowledged and he was practically cut dead at Sandwich."

The next affront came when Travis was assigned a caddie. "I had one of the worst caddies it had ever been my misfortune to be saddled with," said Travis. "This young man, about 26 years old, was a natural-born idiot, and cross-eyed at that. He was too nervous to think of performing the customary duty of teeing a ball, and rarely knew where it went on any shot."

After his first practice round with the incompetent caddie, Travis tried to get another one but was rebuffed. Later, as he marched through the opposition in match play, Travis would repeatedly request the caddie of his vanquished opponent. But at every turn, the caddiemaster had an excuse as to why that was impossible.

For his first tour of the links, Travis took only a putting cleek he had purchased at North Berwick and a few golf balls—a technique that produced the desired effect. "From the first ball I struck I knew I was on the road to recovery. For the first time in two weeks I could "feel" the ball. The necessary "touch" and the resulting "timing" were there, in such sharp contra-distinction to the entire absence of these vitally important essentials previously, that I was at once transported into the golfer's seventh heaven of delight," Travis wrote.

The part of his game that wasn't coming around in time for the championship was his ground game—and since putting was one of his primary talents, without it he knew he was doomed. When all else failed, Edward Phillips, one of the board of strategy members, suggested that Travis try a putter that inventor Arthur T. Knight of the General Electric Company of Schenectady, New York had given to him. Phillips had offered it to Travis previously, but he had refused it on the grounds that it wasn't a golf weapon. This time, though, Phillips insisted, saying, "Certainly it can't behave any worse than your own putter."

Travis could not refute this statement and so he tried it less than 24 hours before his first match. It was love at first sight. Travis felt his confidence flooding back into his body as he rammed putt after putt into the bottom of the cup with the center-shafted Schenectady

The caddie in the background—who Travis was stuck with
no matter how bitterly he complained—almost
cost him the British Amateur.

The putting style that amazed the British at Sandwich in 1904.

putter. So began a relationship for which Travis would be known during the rest of his days.

As the board of strategy gathered on the final night before the competition, Travis was determined. Like many athletes who can turn adversity into inspiration, Travis had talked himself into believing he was fortunate the English had treated him so poorly. "A reasonable number of fleas is good for a dog," he told his friends. "It keeps a dog from forgetting that he is a dog." Upon reflection he later added, "Of course there had been present before a determination to win, but that was as nothing to the now steel-clad resolution to do so."

Some of the better British players received a bye in the first round, but Travis was not so fortunate. Out he went against H. Holden of Royal Liverpool in the morning round. While the weather had been warm and calm for the practice rounds, on the opening Tuesday morning of the competition it began raining at 8 a.m. and poured from 10 a.m. until noon. Travis made a strong start and ran down some lengthy putts with the Schenectady, taking an early lead. At the seventh hole, Travis called Holden for soling his club in a sand bunker and the remainder of the match was played in a contentious atmosphere.

Travis eventually won 4 and 3. When he exited the course at 10 minutes before 2:00, he was soaked all the way through his woolen clothes. Never a big fan of playing in the rain, Travis asked an official if his afternoon match could be delayed while he changed his clothes but his request was denied. He had but 20 minutes to towel himself off in the hallway and make it to the first tee for his afternoon contest.

His opponent, James Robb—runner-up in the 1897 and 1900 playings—was fresh as a daisy, thanks to the default of his morning opponent. The outward half was even, but once again Travis got the Schenectady working on the inward half. An incident occurred at the 11th that—had it not been for a show of good sportsmanship by the Brit—could have affected the outcome. As Travis said, "I had laid my approach putt dead. My caddie was holding the flag and did not understand Mr. Robb's request to take the flagstick out, Mr. Robb being away at the edge of the green, but understood it as a request to pick up my ball, which, to my indignant astonishment, he was in the act of doing when I burst in with, 'What the devil are you doing?' whereupon the ball was instantly replaced and the incident was closed as far as Mr. Robb and I were concerned."

The incident unnerved Travis who lost the next hole before righting himself on the inward half and taking a two-up lead with three to play. Robb halved 16 and won the next, but Travis eked out a half on the home green for a 1-up victory—a victory that would turn out to be his closest encounter of the championship.

This time Travis pleaded vehemently for relief from his caddie's incompetence, but once again he was refused. Board of strategy member Simeon Ford calmed him, advising "the nuisance is probably a mascot," and Travis acquiesced—resigned to conquering this added challenge.

Though the two wins caused consternation in the British camp, many still felt Travis to be an annoying insect that would be swatted away by one of the remaining homegrown talents. After all, Harold Hilton, Horace Hutchinson, John Ball, Bernard Darwin, and Robert Maxwell were some of the stalwarts that the British fans looked to, to stop the invader in his tracks.

Day two dawned warm and sunny and Emmet was getting his wish as the normal wind was docile as the golfers approached the course. Travis played A.W. Murray, and the latter took an early lead by winning the first two holes and having the next pair, but Travis fought back and captured four straight, so that despite losing the ninth he stood one-up at the turn. When he closed Murray out 3 and 1, Travis stood as the only American left in the competition—W.W. Burton of Ekwanok, J. Williamson of Richmond, and Dev Emmet of Garden City were all eliminated.

"The fourth round, against the ex-Irish champion, Mr. H.E. Reade, was the hardest match I had," noted Travis. He never led in the match until the 17th hole. In fact, through much of it he was two down. That was the case by the fourth, with Travis squaring it at the 11th. He was two down again when they arrived at the 15th tee.

On the lengthy 15th, Travis made a fine four and went one down. At the par-3 16th, Travis nailed a 180-yard tee ball to 12 feet and sunk the putt to get back to even. After Reade missed his putt for a four on the 17th, Travis holed his and went one up. The 18th was halved, and with only 14 strokes on the last four holes, Travis had done it again. Now the Brits were *really* concerned. They reasoned, however, that eventually his short drives that had been just barely

Even with his deadly accuracy, Travis failed to hit all the
fairways at Royal St. George's.

clearing the high dunes would fall in, and that the lengthy putts propelled by that croquet mallet that were dropping in the cup would slide by. They also knew that he would face Harold Hilton—twice British Open and British Amateur champion, and arguably the best amateur player in the world—in his next match.

The board of strategy knew just how to handle their man in the evenings. According to Herb Wind in *The Story of American Golf:* "To take his mind off the game, they played cribbage with him and fed him large portions of stout. To keep him on his toes, they extolled the abilities of Hilton and his other possible opponents." They pointed out the drubbing he had taken at Hilton's hands when they played in 1901, and then they fed him more stout.

The next day the wind was up, it was drizzling and even worse weather was threatening. Nevertheless, Travis roared from the starting blocks and swept the first three holes. His handlers smiled. Hilton won the 11th and Travis took it personally, winning the next three holes in a row to end the match 5 and 4, the final shot being a 150-yard iron that came to rest a foot from the hole. Travis finished early and patiently awaited the outcome of the Horace Hutchinson/Robert Maxwell battle. Well past his prime in 1904, Hutchinson had lost the previous year to Maxwell by 7 and 5, but the veteran was playing well and the grueling match went to an extra hole where Hutchinson prevailed.

Though Hutchinson's win was a popular one, the informed spectators knew that Maxwell probably had a better chance of stopping the American, especially considering the toll the morning match took on Hutchinson. Hutchinson said later, "I started out in the afternoon without the smallest idea in life that I was to be beaten by 'that American.' But I had not played two shots before I knew that all of the best of the fight had been taken out of me by that stiff morning match."

"Few of us who watched thought that Mr. Hutchinson would win, and he was beaten by four and two," wrote Henry Leach. This despite the fact that Travis faltered on the inward half, posting two sixes and giving Hutchinson multiple opportunities, all of which he failed to capitalize on. He would now face Ted Blackwell in the final.

More of the same medicine greeted Travis that evening with his friends, including a review of Ted Blackwell's driving accomplishments. Blackwell was quite possibly the longest hitter on the planet

Travis drives in his semifinal match against Horace Hutchinson.

at the time, and had been known to wallop a guttie ball 358 yards on one occasion. Downwind, he had driven St. Andrews' 18th green from the tee, and it was clear he was about to outdrive Travis on every hole of their 36-hole encounter. Somehow, Travis wasn't worried.

Will the Training Pay Off?

The final day was sunny and calm and the enthusiastic crowd of 300 spectators eagerly awaited the start of the morning round. The *London Times* said simply, "Mr. Blackwell will require his very best game to win today." Blackwell knew he carried the golfing honor of Britain on his shoulders.

Both men were nervous on the first tee—Travis won the opener with a bogey to Blackwell's double. "Blackwell was outplayed from the beginning," wrote Taylor who was part of the gallery for the match. "I make the seemingly strange assertion that he lost the match at the very first hole. He pushed his tee shot into the deep rough and Travis poked his up the middle, played short of the guarding bunker for a certain five. Blackwell then committed a bad error of judgment by trying to make unnecessary distance, with the result that he whipped the ball sharply round to the left and into the rough on the other side, making the getting of a five most improbable. Travis won the hole, jumping straight into the lead, which he never lost; as if to remind Blackwell that such errors are costly even at the start of a match." Travis took the second by playing safe on the fairway and then draining a 40-foot putt—the crowd was stunned to see his putting touch still intact for the final. They halved the third, but Travis grabbed the fourth and fifth. Suddenly, Blackwell was four down. He was worried about his chances and angry that despite outdriving Travis by 50 yards or more, he couldn't win a single hole. Travis was obviously calmed by his quick start and later wrote, "In the final against Mr. Blackwell, I had a comfortable feeling all through, and after the first few holes had been played I felt perfectly certain of winning."

When Travis missed a short putt on the sixth—his first falter of the day—there was applause. Blackwell noticed the discourteous behavior and held up his hand to have the gallery stop. "Some day I hope I may entirely forget all recollection of the slight cheering which greeted that failure," Travis said later.

Blackwell fought back and had an opportunity to cut the lead to one on the 13th. He had played two strong woods into the wind and was a short pitch away on the par-5. Meanwhile, Travis was more than 100 yards further back. But The Old Man played a low boring long-iron to birdie range, while Blackwell badly hooked a short iron and frittered away the advantage. Travis added another win before lunch and stood four up after the morning round.

Travis exhibited a casual and confident attitude between the matches, doing a bit of chipping after a relaxed lunch. When he played his worst hole of the championship and took seven on the first contest of the afternoon, the Brits thought the end was near for the American. But Travis came right back to win the second, and three more soon thereafter, to stand six up with 12 left. Blackwell reduced the lead to four, could do no better than to halve the remainders until he ran out of holes, falling to Walter J. Travis 4 up with 3 to play.

"I remember as well as if it were yesterday the scene when Mr. Travis had holed out for the last time on the fifteenth green and become the champion," wrote Henry Leach 13 years later. "It was a beautiful afternoon, the sun was shining warmly, there was the distant murmur of the sea, and overhead the larks were singing in a loud chorus. After the last putt had been holed there was a tense silence for a moment, and then a man near me exclaimed fervently, 'Well, I'm damned!' And that was just it. The procession wound its way to the clubhouse, and all was over."

Not quite. Travis was made to suffer one more indignation at the hands of Lord Northbourne, the presenter of the Cup, whose family had inhabited the castle on the hill above the course for a century, but who knew little about golf. Northbourne spoke for nearly an hour, starting with the Roman occupation of the county of Kent, and rambling on through British history. Eventually, he complemented the British golfers and finally uttered a terse congratulation to Travis. This was followed by a comment that Travis noted was "indelibly engraved on my memory." The Lord said, "Never, never since the days of Caesar has the British nation been subjected to such humiliation, and we fervently hope that history may not repeat itself."

Travis made the briefest of speeches, gracefully accepting the trophy, applauding the fine play of the British amateurs and concluding by saying, "I am hopelessly bunkered. I pick up my ball."

The press was nearly unanimous in its praise for Travis. Even the British *Golf Illustrated* said in part: "Each competitor who had to face the American champion during the week came out of the ordeal

Travis was determined, no matter what the
predicament at Sandwich.

with a chastened respect for the steady game and great pertinacity
of the man, and above all with a high admiration of his powers on
the putting green. Mr. Travis' putting in the final match was nothing
short of marvelous." Blackwell agreed, and was quoted as saying,
"Travis is a great golfer. He deserved to win. I was a trifle off my
game during the morning and lost several holes I ought to have won.
The strain told on me."

At home, *The New York Times* marveled: "No international sporting event for a long time has created the widespread interest that has been excited by Travis's victory. Travis may now justly be called the amateur golf champion of the world."

Horace Hutchinson was also gracious in defeat and appreciative of Travis's talent. "Everyone is asking—have you seen that American who is putting with an extraordinary thing like a croquet mallet and putting extraordinarily well? With that long black cigar in his mouth and his deliberate methods, including the practice swing before each stroke, he is a rather hard man to play against. I think critics make a mistake who say he is not a first class golfer."

Board of strategy member Simeon Ford led the cheer when the Americans were in private. He later penned a humorous article for *Country Life in America* titled "How Me and Travis Won the Golf Championship." "To four things may be attributed Travis' success. First and foremost was the influence of that trainer, guide, mentor and friend whose peerless eloquence is now electrifying you. With all becoming modesty I assert that I was quite a factor in the result. In the first place, constant association with me goaded him into such a state of madness that he simply had to go out and lick some one. And then he made a careful study of my golfing style, and by carefully eliminating everything I did he attained perfection. Then there was that magical putter, borrowed of a friend the day before the tourney. It came from Schenectady, and it was a bird with salt on its tail. And then there was the magic black dope cigar which strengthened Travis and at the same time weakened his adversity. Really, I think the cigar had a lot to do with it. To see his opponent try to work out to windward of him made you think of the Cup races. But Travis would get the weather gauge on him, hold him under his lee, belch forth clouds of dense black miasmatic vapor, and his man would get green 'round the gills and his eyes would run, and the sweat would start, and his game would fade away, and it was all over."

There were some who thought part of the magic lay in the cigar and made inquiries as to what brand the champion smoked. But more of immediate concern to the Brits was the practical matter of that strange putter. Club pro Tom Vardon made a large special order for the implements and by the week's end, the supply was exhausted. One of the purchasers was Ted Blackwell. Everyone knew there must be some unexplained magic that resided in the wand.

Putting stance and grip from his book, *The Art of Putting.*

"If there had been any luke-warmness on the part of the Sandwich people," Travis later wrote, "this was more than compensated for by the friendly attitude of the Cinque Ports Golf Club at Deal, right next door to Sandwich. A dinner was given to 'foreign invaders' at the invitation of Mr. James Leslie Wanklyn, M.P., captain of the Cinque Ports Golf Club, at the Union Club, adjoining the Castle at Deal, on the Saturday evening following the championship and the freedom of the course was ours."

Travis received a flood of telegrams after his triumph including congratulations from the members at Garden City and The Country Club in Brookline, as well as personal wishes from George Orvis, Laidlaw Purves, and Rhona Adair. Mr. Sheldon in New York asked "What does Hilton think of your game now?" and Mr. Kingsley commented, "Your success makes every golfer in America stand a little straighter and brings hope to those of the brotherhood who are no longer boys." In a show of class, the captains and members of Royal Liverpool Golf Club sent their hearty congratulations. In the reverse, Doubleday asked, "Can't you send feature article 2000 words and photographs early next week?"

Travis also received a letter from Andrew Carnegie at Skibo Castle in Dornoch, which began, "Now you are among the Immortals." Carnegie extolled the virtues of Royal Dornoch, calling it "the best in Scotland taking scenery and climate into account," and tried to lure Travis to visit and stay with him.

But Travis had committed to play in the British Open, which was to follow the amateur by a week at Sandwich. He honored his commitment but his heart wasn't in it, and he was ready to put England behind him. Arriving back in New York on June 21, Travis said of the Open, "It seemed as though I could not get myself worked up to take any deep interest in my play." Reflecting on the previous events of the trip, Travis continued, "You might add that a very great deal of my success is due to the encouragement and support of the Yankee gallery we had with us. Simeon Ford as a trainer is a big success."

When asked if he would go back given the treatment he received, Travis said "Next year the meeting is at Prestwick, the best of the five championship courses. At present I have no intention of going across, much as I should like to."

The Editor

Walter Travis and the
Schenectady Putter

From the moment he won the 1904 British Amateur, Walter Travis's name has always been associated with the Schenectady putter— a device he did not design (as many people believe), and a weapon that was just one of the many putters he used during his career.

A day before the British Amateur, when his putting was in the gutter and Travis was in despair about his chances in the tournament, Edward Phillips—one of his traveling companions and a member at the Mohawk Golf Club in Schenectady, New York—handed him a Schenectady putter and encouraged him to try it. When the ball started finding the hole with regularity, Travis slid the club in his bag. Over the next four days, he used it to dispense with Horace Hutchinson, Harold Hilton, Ted Blackwell, and several others en route to his stunning victory—a win the Brits attributed to the center-shafted, mallet-headed device, one which was relatively unknown in Great Britain.

But Travis had already employed the Schenectady at the 1902 U.S. Open at Garden City, so the odd-looking device was not an alien in his hands. The putter was originally developed by Arthur T. Knight of Schenectady, an employee of General Electric since 1897 and a member of Mohawk at its inception just a year later. Knight was an accomplished player who wished to play number one on the Mohawk team, but often fell victim to better putting by others. Knight designed a wooden version of the putter in 1901 and filled a back cavity with molten lead, but the feel wasn't right. He later cast the head in aluminum and asked Jimmy Thompson, the pro at Mohawk to build him a few in 1902. Knight then loaned one to Phillips, who showed it around at Garden City and got Devereux Emmet and others interested in the odd design.

Emmet wrote to Knight on August 21, 1902, saying in part: "With your permission I will play with it and show it at Garden City and Myopia where I am going and will then send it back to you. I would advise you to patent it immediately as I am confident that you will sell a lot of them when they become known."

Travis employed the putter with success at the Open, but then it fell into personal disfavor and was replaced in his bag by another implement. He did write to Knight on October 12, 1902, the day after the Open saying, "Will you please send to Mr. R. Watson Jr. a putter similar to mine, with bill, and he will remit. He would prefer dull finish to nickel." Watson was the secretary of the USGA at the time, and Travis's request was in part to validate the club in the eyes of the governing body.

Knight took Emmet's advice, especially since the Spalding Company was planning to market their version of the instrument in 1903. The putter was patented on March 24, 1903, with an aluminum alloy head, rather than the wood version with brass faceplate that was produced afterward. The originals, and especially a few that are engraved with 'Patent Pending,' bring a substantial price in today's collectible club market.

Others heard of Travis's success with the implement, and soon Knight was swimming in orders. In June of 1903, Knight traveled to Baltusrol to talk with both Travis and Emmet at the U.S. Open. Knight was anxious to call the stick the Travis putter and so he approached Travis with an offer. While not declining the use of his name, Travis convinced him that the putter was already well-known as the Schenectady, and the distinctive name would serve object and maker well. Knight reluctantly agreed.

The putter found some converts, but was not well-known until Travis beat the Brits with it at Royal St. George's in Sandwich. It then enjoyed a smashing success with numerous versions produced until the Royal and Ancient reviewed the matter early in 1910. Asked to rule on a question posed by the Nga Motu Golf Club of New Zealand regarding croquet mallet use for putting, the august body stated that "a croquet mallet is not a putter and is inadmissible."

In response, the Pickering Golf Club in England asked for clarification regarding all mallet-headed putters. In May of 1910, the chairman of the Rules Committee, W.H. Burn, suggested the following motion: "That the Rules of Golf Committee be empowered to add to the clause on the Form and Make of Golf Clubs words which shall declare that all clubs with heads of the mallet-type are a substantial departure from the traditional form and make of golf clubs." Burn's suggestion was adopted and, much to the consternation of committee member Charles Blair Macdonald, the Schenectady was banned.

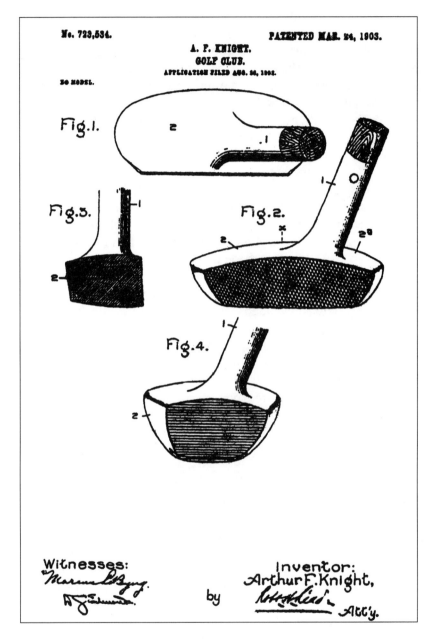

There have been many variations on the center-shafted putter. Travis used the original Arthur Knight model, patented in 1903.

Without any input into the R&A ruling, but not supporting the ban on the Schenectady, the USGA was now confronted with a dilemma. Not since agreeing on cooperation regarding the rules had there been such a schism between the governing bodies. Travis, of course had an opinion on the matter, and by 1911, as editor of *The American Golfer,* he also had a bully pulpit from which to pontificate. "The USGA has always been loyal to St. Andrews, even at a time when domestic troubles were uppermost and when there was imminent danger of a complete breaking away." But Travis called for the USGA to stand on its own in this matter and cited several examples of instances where the rules of the two organizations already differed. One—that the USGA allowed practice swings and the R&A had banned them—explains Horace Hutchinson noting the difficulty of playing against Travis, who, contrary to Scottish custom (but not yet a rule in 1904) always made a practice swing before hitting his shot. Travis noted that permitting the Schenectady "would meet with unqualified approval by American golfers generally." He couldn't help himself when he added, "And we will go a step farther and venture the opinion that outside a small coterie in Great Britain it would also commend itself to British golfers."

At a meeting in Chicago in January of 1911, according to *Golf Illustrated,* "It was agreed to support the Royal and Ancient rule to the effect that no departure from the traditional and accepted form and make of golf clubs could be sanctioned, but the interpretation of this rule was left to the executive committee, with the instructions that they should interpret it in such a way as not to bar the Schenectady putter."

In April of 1920, Travis was approached by Spalding regarding the manufacture of a Schenectady-style putter bearing the name "Travis Putter." Travis tinkered with the design, inserting lead in the head and equipping it with a stiff shaft. Spalding modified the design until Travis was happy with it. He gave his approval for limited production on June 29. In July, the putter was still being held up by Spalding's backlog of 50,000 unfilled orders for clubs. Travis took the opportunity to add a sighting line on the top, then wrote that it was "the best putter I ever had." He closed his letter with "When do you expect to turn them out in quantity? I am constantly being asked this question." This showed that the putter was still a popular choice with golfers 15 years after its appearance. When the putter was

Spalding produced a line of Travis clubs for many years.

finally produced late in the summer of 1920, Travis began to receive a royalty of 75 cents per putter sold—a payment that endured beyond his passing.

The R&A held by its decision for 41 years until it finally dropped the prohibition and sided with the American position. By then Travis had long since passed away, other Americans had won the British championship and the sting of that humiliating victory had finally worn off. There were probably some people who regretted the rescinding, however, for just two years later Ben Hogan won the British Open at Carnoustie...with a center-shafted putter.

Searching for Motivation

When Travis returned to America in June of 1904, his life began to change. Despite the jovial mood of his friends on the voyage home, Travis couldn't help feeling disillusioned. He had always cherished the traditions of golf, appreciated its homeland, and written of his respect for British golfers and admiration of the British courses. He had been instrumental in arranging international matches, suffered defeat gracefully at the hands of the Oxford and Cambridge players, and hosted them in the spirit of friendship. He had gone abroad with certain expectations, and although he was happy to have won the championship, he was disappointed with everything else.

Things were changing in America as well. A new generation of golfers was advancing and young men like Jerome Travers, Chandler Egan, Fred Herreshoff, Chick Evans, and Rob Gardner were challenging the Old Man's reign at the top.

Travis himself was changing as well. He was 42 years old, and after only eight seasons of golf he had reached his goal of winning the U.S. Amateur three times. Now, with the British Amateur, came the title of amateur champion of the world and the fulfillment of yet another goal. With these accomplishments in his back pocket, it became harder to put the game face on. It had already been demonstrated that when Travis was motivated he was invincible, but when he was indifferent it showed.

At the Nassau Invitational that summer, Travis met the 17-year-old Jerry Travers for the first time, in what would be a long series of matches throughout the remainder of his career. Travers gives a long account of this encounter in his book, *The Fifth Estate*. He had just dispensed with Douglas Findlay, advancing the farthest he ever had in an event of such prominence, against men of such accomplishments—quite an eye-opener for a kid still in high school. Brimming with renewed confidence, and encouraged by his mentor, host pro Aleck Smith, he immediately fell two down to Travis after three. "I should have wilted under the tension of facing so distinguished an adversary and been crushed under the methodical precision of his shot-making," wrote Travers. "But I wasn't. The ogre of stage fright was missing; the nervous strain, which I came to know only too well in later years, never appeared. Why? I should like to know myself."

Travers fought back, squared the match at number six and went one up at seven. Then the senior rallied and reeled off wins. As they stood on 14 tee, Walter was once again two up. It was there that something clicked for young Jerry.

"The break in this match came at the fourteenth hole. There was every indication that I was beaten. I thought so, the gallery thought so and I am sure Travis was of the same opinion. My opponent, as familiar as he was with the fickleness of golf, seemed to take it for granted that I could not overcome his handicap. There was something about the careless as he played an approach to the 14th green which told me he had decided that I had ceased to be a threat, and the effect of that on me was irritation. It fanned a spark of renewed determination. If I was destined to lose, it could not be said I had not gone down fighting."

Travers won the hole, halved the next two, and tied the match on 17, holding on at the home green to send it to extras. Each golfer had a chance to win on the first two holes, but it was Travers's long birdie putt at the third that iced it—the kid had beaten the old man— in large part due to his motivation when it seemed Travis let his guard down. These two would wage many a memorable battle for the next dozen years at club events, metropolitan championships, and U.S. Amateurs.

In September, Travis entered the U.S. Amateur as the defending champion, but the newspapers were already talking about some of the new sensations. On the day before play began, *The New York Times* said, "H. Chandler Egan, the Western champion, and his cousin Walter E. Egan, both Harvard students, put in a good day's practice yesterday. The former is a powerfully long driver, and is expected to be among the leaders at the finish."

Travis made his quickest exit ever from the championship, winning his first match against Pierre Proal of Seabright 6 and 5, but losing his second to G.A. Ormiston of Oakmont by 3 and 1. Ormiston turned the tables Travis-style by halving the first hole, winning the next two, and never relinquishing the lead thereafter. "Travis took his defeat with the utmost good humor and heartily congratulated Ormiston on his excellent golf," wrote *The Times*. "Travis, as his friends have freely admitted, has not been playing the practically invincible game that has made him a victor in so many hard-fought contests. His golf has been good, but no better than that of at least half a dozen other competitors." As predicted, Chandler Egan was there at the finish, an 8 and 6 winner over Fred Herreshoff, and a new era had begun.

The Art of Putting was published in Great Britain in 1905,
but very few copies were sold.

A Desire to Write

Travis was turning his attention elsewhere, looking around for some jobs in golf course architecture and an outlet for his writing talents. He had written about his win at Sandwich for numerous publications, including *Country Life in America* and *Golf*, and he had contributed articles about the differences between British and American golf for *Vanity Fair* and *Golf Illustrated*. On the latter subject, he held his line about the superiority of the British links and players despite the bad taste in his mouth after the championship. He wrote: "At the outset I am perfectly free to confess that you have very many more first-class players than we have—probably twenty to one. Golf in America is played under more disadvantageous circumstances than in Great Britain. In the first place, courses on your side are, generally, much better."

Travis was also asked to contribute to a second book—a deal that was hammered out with the London-based Macmillan Company. The book was a collaboration between himself and the Open champion, Jack White, who was crowned a week after the amateur at Sandwich, and the title was *The Art of Putting*. Each man was to describe his technique and mental processes on the putting surface. Photographs were taken at the site by George Beldam, and the 31-page book was hurried into production to take advantage of the recent victories. Unlike *Practical Golf*, which was long, detailed and a reflection of Travis through and through, this offering was short, sketchy and not how Travis conceived it. The book might have been more popular overseas had Travis putted brilliantly but not won the championship. But there was scorn for the man who took the cup to America—the book was a commercial failure and few copies were printed, making it a highly sought-after book among collectors today.

The New Generation

Just after the first of the year, Travis took a golfing excursion to Bermuda with Macdonald. At the time Bermuda had three nine-hole courses and Travis quickly set the course record at St. George's, going around in a mere 32 strokes. In a four-ball, Travis teamed with local scratch player Major Bigge. The first day, they were beaten by Macdonald and A.L. Norris of Dyker Meadow. They had their revenge the next day, winning 4 up with 2 to play.

In another superstar contest, Travis beat the best ball of Macdonald and professional Horace Rawlins. But in the following match, once again the former day's losers were winners. Bermudans were awed by the sophistication of the play, but Travis and Macdonald saved their biggest trick for last—playing the best ball of six soldiers—and beating them. Unimpressed by this dog and pony show, *Golf* magazine commented, "There is some novelty on account of the numbers, but when you are vastly superior you might as well play sixty as six."

In 1905, a small and clever book written by John Hogben of Edinburgh under the pseudonym Cleeke Shotte and titled *The Golf Craze; Sketches and Rhymes* appeared. Hogben paid tribute to Travis with a short verse.

> *The cry is still "They come!" for we may say*
> *The lust of conquest reigns in U.S.A.*
> *Another Cup goes Westward; 'tis a shock*
> *We owe, sir, to that aluminum block*
> *They taught your golf ball all roads lead to Rome.*
> *And sent it straight, and far, and surely home.*
> *There is no name whereby to call the utter*
> *Amazement that we owe to your strange putter.*

Travis began 1905 with an article in *Country Life of America* titled "Changes in the Game of Golf." The headline was a reference to his recent conversion from the 43-inch driver that most players used at the time, to a 50-inch weapon. He claimed that by simply standing further from the ball, shortening his backswing and exaggerating his

Travis experimented with drivers as long as 52 inches.

follow-through he could swing the long-shafted clubs and gain 10 yards on each drive.

Jason Rogers, golf editor of the *New York Globe* wrote, "The long-shafted golf club now used by Mr. Travis is the chief topic of conversation these days whenever golfers meet. Every golfer is desirous of securing the greatest possible distance consistent with accuracy on his full shots, and therefore the entire golfing world is watching the experiments of Mr. Travis."

Golf magazine reported the lengths of clubs to be used in 1905 by all the top players, and followed the progress of every round Travis played at Garden City with the club, including one that began with an outward 34. One article detailed the length of every tee ball and where every shot landed. Travis concluded: "I find that a somewhat longer ball can be secured with the longer club, but it is at the expense of a certain measure of accuracy. Still, although it may not be advisable to use constantly the more powerful, but slightly more erratic weapon, there are occasions when it is a mighty good club to have in one's bag." It is unclear how long Travis played the long shaft, but later in the season Alex Smith and Willie Anderson were swinging 51-inchers, and Stewart Gardner was hefting 48.

Elsewhere in the article, Travis wrote of the fine showing made by the American contingent in the British Amateur in 1904 and that if the Oxford and Cambridge Golfing Society would return, he was sure the American team could give them a better game. Travis also talked about the future of American golf. He saw that golf had arrived as a solid part of the American social scene—10 years after its initial exposure—and that it undoubtedly would appeal to all classes of people in the future. He thought that "the American spirit" would help us to play better in "half the time that it would take an English player to arrive at the same stage."

Travis also made note of the next generation of players who were nipping at the heels of the established guard like himself. "It is extremely difficult to foretell if there are any great surprises in store for us in the way of budding champions blossoming forth later on and ousting the present leaders—and maintaining their superiority. One or two of the younger generation of players gave evidence last season of possessing latent possibilities, which, properly developed, should make them very dangerous antagonists. The greater opportunities for more frequent play afforded to the younger players should certainly result in the gradual displacement of the older players who do not enjoy such favorable opportunities."

His 1904 win in the British Amateur was the subject of much ridicule in the British papers.

A Pinehurst Story

By the next time Travis entered the North and South, a second course had been added at Pinehurst. Primarily installed for women, the Number 2 course was not getting the play it deserved. "For several years I have been at Mr. Tufts, the proprietor, to make this an exacting test. The course was originally designed for ladies. The distances on the holes were fairly good and capable of extension, but there wasn't a single bunker. It was so tame and insipid that there was practically no play over it. Everyone preferred the number one course, which, comparatively speaking had some teeth to it," noted Travis.

"The suggestion did not meet with favor. Mr. Tufts had an idea that the class of player who visited Pinehurst did not want anything severe. I thought otherwise. Finally in 1906 I won him around to my way of thinking and he gave me carte blanche to go ahead. I knew the changes that I had in mind would result in a big uproar at the start, and I didn't feel like shouldering the whole responsibility. So I suggested that Donald Ross and I should go over the course together and, without conferring, each propose a separate plan. I knew what the result would be.

"For some time I had been pouring into Donald's ears my ideas; in point of fact, I had urged him to take on the laying out of courses, as with the certain development of the game a fine future was assured for one having a bent in this line. In those days Willie Dunn had ceased to figure and his successor, although credited with laying out hundreds of courses all over the country, really had no genius for the work. Donald heeded my advice...and golf has been tremendously benefited by his many fine creations since." (That last sentence was a slam at Tom Bendelow, the designer of Oakland Golf Club, where Travis learned the game.)

Travis was codifying his ideas on design, and believed that America was ready to make a move from what he termed the "Willie Dunn system." "His method was simply to select a suitable site for the putting green and to put in a cross bunker for the tee shot and another cross bunker for the second shot. Not only were they offensively artificial, lacking wholly in artistic finish, but they placed all players on a dead level of equality. They rarely troubled the fairly long hitter, but they were a terrible trial to the weak player."

Travis claimed that at this juncture, Ross was "merely an echo of my own views regarding the fundamental principles of golf course architecture. Whereas the Willie Dunn system called for compulsory carries for both tee and second shots, I was an advocate of optional carries; that is to say, I believe in the principle of giving a player a choice of carrying a bunker or playing safe. But if he elected to play safe on the tee shot, he would be confronted with the same problem on the second shot. In other words, I simply cut Dunn's cross bunkers in half, now to the right and again to the left.

"So I felt quite certain of what would happen. Donald and I were a unit. And the course was bunkered accordingly, with one exception, and that was on the twelfth hole. Here I planned three avenues of play, down the middle, narrow with a big bunker 180 yards from the tee, leaving a clear second to the green. It was quite revolutionary in those days, such a big carry, but it was decided to construct the holes as outlined. When he came to it, however, Donald's courage failed him; he weakly compromised by making a straightaway affair of it, with a bunker at the right some 160 yards from the tee, which didn't mean anything."

Nevertheless, much of what turned Pinehurst Number 2 into the course it is today, was, according to Travis in a 1920 *American Golfer* article, his work and his plans. Since both Ross and Tufts were still alive when the claim was made, and neither of them stepped forward to refute it, the boast must have been based in some measure of reality.

"What was the result of this stiffening up?" Travis continues. "Men who ordinarily did number one course in the lower 80s tackled number two. Up ran their scores in the high 90s, possibly over the century mark. Disgusted, they emphatically declared they were through—it was a course only for experts. But—and here lies the lure of the game, challenging the player to match his skill against difficulties—a little sober reflection, pique, never-say-die, or something or other rushed those same men over to number two the first thing the following day, in a laudable effort, also mostly vain, to beat that 97 of the previous day. And at it they kept day after day.

"Whereas the problem had been how to get players from number one to number two, now a new one presented itself—how to get

Putting at the College Arms course in Deland, Florida.

them back to number one—which was finally solved in a way by stiffening up number one."

Although Travis was turning his attention more and more to writing and golf course architecture, by no means did he completely turn his back on competition. He started 1906 with two wins in Florida—first capturing the Florida Amateur by beating Charles Cory by 5 and 4, and then taking the Florida Open at Palm Beach against a field filled with foreign professionals—including Andrew Kirkaldy, Alec Herd, Arthur Fenn, Roland Jones, and Percy Barret.

Though he may not have been the awe-inspiring combatant he once was, Travis remained competitive for another decade, much to the amazement of the younger players. And while he would never win another U.S. Amateur, he did finish as the medalist another three times—in 1906, 1907, and 1908. As Herb Wind wrote in *The Story of American Golf,* "He could play superb golf for two or three rounds—rather similar to the way Bill Tilden, after he reached fifty, could still hold his own with any tennis player for one set. But the Old Man's stamina was failing, and toward the end of the tournament week the youngsters could take him."

In 1906, the Amateur was played in July at the Englewood Golf Club in New Jersey and Travis rolled through his first two opponents

Travis generated power by squaring himself to the
target during his extended follow-through.

before confronting Jerry Travers in the quarterfinals. Disposing of
his young nemesis 3 and 2, it looked as if Travis had a chance at the
title, only to be derailed by Eben Byers by 4 and 3 in the semis.

Travis got his revenge for that defeat just a few months later in
an invitational at the Myopia Hunt Club. Travis and Byers marched
through their halves of the draw, consisting mainly of Myopia members, and squared off in a 36-hole final. In typical Travis style, the
Old Man grabbed control of the match with wins on the second and
third holes and never looked back, winning 6 and 5.

Travis considered Myopia the best course in the country and he
stated this clearly and often—first in a November 1905 article in
Country Life: "As a whole it is beyond criticism. No two holes are

alike, and there is not a single hole which is in any way unfair or which does not call for good play. The charm of the course lies in its diversity, the excellence of the lengths of each hole, the physical characteristics, the well-conceived system of hazards, good lies throughout, tees better than most putting greens, and putting greens, mostly undulating, which are the finest in the country and equal to the best anywhere in the world."

Six months later, Travis expanded on his previous pronounce-ment, this time framing it with his impressions of British golf courses. In the article, Travis cites all his favorite holes on the preferred links of Scotland and England, adding, "Our courses are, for the most part, laid out on the same dead level of comparatively uninteresting uniformity, the one notable exception being Myopia."

Travis extols the virtues of natural hazards, bunkers with a di-versity of appearance, undulating linksland with great variety in el-evation, routings that never become monotonous with side-by-side, back-and-forth companion holes and allowing alternate paths to the putting surface. He lambastes cross bunkers that punish the less accomplished, flat greens that fail to test the ground game and green committees who have not seen the models they should be emulat-ing. "What a splendid thing it would be if the green committees of our leading clubs would only take a trip abroad and make a peregri-nation of the principal links, and see, for themselves, what real golf links are like."

In some ways, it was a tribute to Travis that he could continue to rave about the links of a land where he was so scorned. The British press continued to take potshots at him, two years after his win, including the accusation that he wrecked their trophy. In a July 27, 1906, letter to the British *Golf Illustrated*, buddy Simeon Ford was forced to rise to his defense. "My attention has just been drawn to the enclosed clipping from the *Sunday Times*, which would seem to intimate that our friend Travis had been guilty of abusing the cup which he won at Sandwich. I was with Travis when the cup arrived (by Express—charges not prepaid). It was in a leather case, loosely packed, and looked rather the worse for wear and tear. It looked as though infants might have been teething on it, or as if some previous holder had used a niblick not wisely, but too well upon it. We packed it carefully, and on arrival at New York, Travis sent it to our leading silversmith, where it was put in shape. It was then turned over to

Travis's home club, the Garden City G.C., and the secretary at once put it in a safe deposit vault, where it remained until it was shipped back to Albion's shore. From my own acquaintance with Travis I feel sure that he neither pawned it nor used it for a cooking utensil, but I fear poor Walter will never be forgiven for his audacity in winning that much envied nightmare in silver. But we who know him and admire him as a good golfer and thorough sportsman hate to see such nasty digs as he gets occasionally in English papers."

Groundbreaking Writings

Travis was also one of the leading—if not only—writers of the day in the field of golf course maintenance. His detailed chapter on putting greens in *Practical Golf* was one of the foremost descriptions of the subject when it first appeared in 1901, and he continued to add to the literature through his experience at Garden City. In 1906, he contributed a chapter to a book by Leonard Barron titled *Lawn Making* and subtitled *Together with the Proper Keeping of Putting Greens*. Published by Doubleday, Doran & Co. in 1906, it was republished in 1929 for the National Garden Association, achieving a wider audience even after Travis's passing. He added articles for *Country Life* and *Golf* on maintaining and improving putting surfaces—something that wasn't getting much press during this time—and the following provides the essence of his thoughts on establishing a green in 1906:

"Plough up the surface to a depth of a foot or so and remove all loose material," Travis began. "Then proceed to fill in a layer of sand a few inches in depth and cover it with good loam about an inch or so thick; on top of this put a thin crust of well-rotted manure, and then another layer of loam of two or three inches. At this stage apply a dressing of bone-dust, with a touch of slacked lime. Cover this with a suggestion of sand, superficially only, and top off with loam, the surface being raked and finely pulverized. Sow liberally with a mixture of re-cleaned Red Top, Rhode Island Bent, Creeping Bent, Crested Dog's Tail and Kentucky Bluegrass, and level off and roll with a very light roller."

Travis suggested abundant moisture to grow the surface in and carefully removing all weeds and coarse grass by the roots. Then, "well-rotted manure is a good plant food, in conjunction with bone-dust. Pulverized sheep manure is also excellent and a slight sprinkling of wood-ashes will do no harm. Avoid, however, any over-indulgence in potash fertilizers, as they provoke a growth of clover, and clover has no place on a course. Unless it is kept very closely cut on the greens, it has a very 'draggy' and retarding effect on the run of a ball, and is therefore undesirable.

"The ideal putting green is covered with a close sward of very fine grass, with a thick matting of roots. The blades should be fine and slender, silky yet tenacious—entirely different from the ordinary first-class lawn. A coarse, large-bladed grass, the product of undue fertility, is not what is wanted—quite the contrary. Putting, in the true sense of the word, is impossible on such."

Travis suggested a regular application of fine sand—a practice that was unheard of outside of St. Andrews—primarily to ward off the most common putting green problem at the century's turn: worm casts. "Concerning worms, it may safely be said that the richer the soil the greater is the wealth of worms, and, inversely, the poorer the soil the greater freedom from this curse. There are some worm mixtures on the market, which are excellent but somewhat expensive. A very good and inexpensive substitute may be found by boiling a couple of bars of ordinary yellow laundry soap, and mixing it with a barrel full of from 30 to 40 gallons of water, applying the mixture freely through an ordinary watering pot. This will bring the worms to the surface in myriads, where they may be easily gathered." It's hard for us to imagine how much of a problem worms were, but given the rich native loams that were being pushed up for greens, it was a perplexing and pervasive problem. On the seaside links of Great Britain worms were not a concern, but few courses in the United States enjoyed a sand-based soil so common overseas.

Travis didn't believe in babying the putting surfaces. "Nothing improves a green so much as being constantly played upon, provided that the holes are frequently changed, before they show any evidence of wear. The human foot is a great agency, and wonderfully assists the work of the roller. Every green should be rolled daily with a light roller—whether it apparently needs it or not." He also did not believe in covering the greens for the winter. "It seems to me that the artificial protection afforded by covering them with manure, straw, or anything else (save a little sand) unfits the grass to withstand the severities of play, especially during the summer months."

Finally, Travis firmly advocates winter play. "It is the common opinion that a green will be irretrievably ruined by playing on it during the winter months. This is a delusion. Observe carefully, at the beginning of spring, the actual condition of temporary greens set apart on many courses for the winter. There is nothing then—or subsequently—to give the slightest indication that the roots have been impaired in the least degree—nor have they."

In conclusion, the man who gained fame through his uncanny putting ability noted, "The proper care of greens demands unceasing care and unremittent, intelligent attention. Eternal vigilance is the price of first-class greens."

As a result of his advice on greens maintenance, Travis received a letter from the New York Golf Club, a group of public golfers who were concerned about the condition of the greens at Van Cortlandt Park and had complained to the Park Department of the City of New York. The Park Department gave them two greens to experiment on, and they were seeking Travis's advice on whether or not they could be made into playable greens. "You can get good greens at Van Cortland Park," wrote Travis in a reply that was carried in *Golf* magazine, "—you can get good greens anywhere." He went on to explain how to completely strip the green of the old grass, level and prepare the surface, plant new grasses and give them the materials they needed to be strong, healthy putting surfaces.

Suggesting Radical Changes

Not content to merely explain how good greens are obtained and what well-laid-out courses should entail, in 1906 Travis also took to trashing American courses that he felt were insufficient and overrated. After panning Fox Hills in the same article that he praised Myopia, Travis then turned to Nassau, where he criticized a third of the holes and the cop bunkers on the remainder—bunkers he claimed marred the beauty of the course. "Properly arranged in irregularly shaped mounds—as could easily have been done in the first instance, or could be done even now—the present cut-and-dried appearance would give way to a more natural—more golfy—look and be more in keeping with the actual playing merits of the course."

Next on the hit list was Baltusrol—and remember this is pre-Tillinghast—which he declared as "being a typical example of nearly everything that is lacking in all the essentials that go to make up a first-class course." He went on to claim that nature never intended the site to be a golf course, that mountain climbing is one thing and golf is another, that the ball frequently performs unexpected stunts due to vagaries in the fairways and approaches and that "I have played there on several occasions, but it has always been my misfortune to find the greens in poor shape." He closes by wondering why the USGA would ever choose the course for one of its championships. It's doubtful the evaluation was very popular at the venerable establishment.

Travis also took a swipe at his home club, which was the beginning of the end of his friendship with Dev Emmet. His article started with "Garden City is one of the best courses in the country," but the next 15 paragraphs were devoted to suggested improvements to nearly every hole. The article then deteriorated into, "As to the greens, the majority are too flat and consequently uninteresting."

This battle was just getting warmed up. By the end of the year the Club commissioned Travis to perform the alterations he was suggesting on four of the holes. If the changes met with approval, the Club would allow him to continue. When Arthur Pottow wrote about the changes for the *Illustrated Outdoor News*, he said: "If they meet with the general approval of the members of the Garden City club, without doubt similar methods will be applied to some, if not all, of the other holes, and then the transformation will be revolutionary indeed. But it will not stop at Garden City. Other courses throughout the country which are ambitious of being admitted into that small, but select, circle where class golf is demanded will follow suit, and we shall then see courses which will amaze those who founded golf in this country."

The change Travis envisioned for Garden City was the same change he proposed for Pinehurst. Instead of bunkers crossing the fairway and catching the weakly hit straight ball, have the bunkers line the fairways and catch the strong but off-line tee ball. For many years, Travis was pegged as an architect who advanced a penal style of play. In truth, it was just the opposite. Travis wanted to see a strategic element to infiltrate the layouts, leaving the duffer alone, but challenging the accomplished. At Garden City, he also added pot bunkers in front of the 1st, 12th, and 18th greens. The message was clear: steer clear of these or risk the consequences.

At the second hole, Travis received permission to modify the surface of the green. "Here the putting green has been made to undulate artificially," wrote Pottow. "The turf was taken off the green, ridges smoothed and rounded were raised, and the turf was put back on again. Looking at the green it somewhat resembles the billowy agitation of a stage sea in a nautical play."

The undulating theory was pushed to the limit on the 12th green according to the writer and a "hazard of a distinctly original type" was installed at several holes, including to the left of the 16th green. One writer described it as an "asparagus bed hazard," another likened it to "a dozen huge nutmeg graters laid side by side." Needless to say, the mounds were controversial but Travis would still not be satisfied with the paltry changes. Over the next decade he would head the green committee and then quit and vow to have nothing more to do with it. Later he would be right back in the thick of it, and so it went at his home club into the 1920s.

Throughout all of his writing, golf course architecture work, advising on green construction and competitive career, Travis held down a job outside of golf. When he first moved to the United States it was hardware, then he dabbled in the advertising business before moving on to Waterman, Anthony and Company, a prominent broker on the New York Stock Exchange. Travis was named to head an up-

---

Waterman, Anthony & Co.
67 Exchange Place, :: New York
BANKERS & BROKERS

Members of the
New York Stock Exchange
New York Cotton Exchange

¶ Orders carefully executed
for the purchase and sale of
stocks for cash or on margin

Branch Office, No. 5 West 58th St.
Walter J. Travis, *Manager*

When he left McLean Bros & Rigg Hardware, Travis managed a
branch office for Waterman, Anthony and Co. in New York.

town office, scheduled to open in the Plaza Hotel at 5 West 58th
Street on March 1, 1907. He would not remain there long.

In July 1907, the Amateur was held at the Euclid Club in Cleveland and once again Travis was the medalist. The newspapers had
picked up on a story—and *The New York Times* was about to run it
on the front page the next day—that Travis had refused to shake the
congratulatory hand of John D. Rockefeller. Travis wrote to Anne
from the Union Club in Cleveland where he was staying to assure
her the story was groundless, and that he intended to wire the press,
"The report that I declined to shake hands with Mr. Rockefeller is a
pure unadulterated lie. On the contrary, I have had that pleasure on
three occasions." He went on to say, "Won the medal today. Playing
well—and for the first time in a long while, I'm fired with the desire
to win. I'm really going to try."

Once again Travis easily defeated his first two opponents by
identical 3 up with 2 to play scores, eliminating Thomas Sherman of
Sadaquada and George Lyon of Lambton, before meeting W.C.
Fownes of Oakmont in the semifinals. "The sensation of the day was

the defeat of Walter Travis by the Pittsburgh golfer, W.C. Fownes," wrote the *Times* reporter. "History repeated itself. Two years ago, in the play for the championship over the Chicago Golf Club links at Wheaton, Illinois, Fownes put Travis out of the running in an extra hole match in the third round of play, as was the case today."

Apparently the 'old fire' was no longer quite enough.

Salisbury Links

In the summer and fall of 1907, Travis was involved in the design of a new golf course in Garden City. It had been eight years since he had plotted Ekwanok. In the interim he had seen hundreds of courses, won four major championships, twice visited the greatest links of Britain, written dozens of articles, and had the urge to design a golf course that would showcase the theorems he was espousing. But the only work he had done was remodeling and suggesting.

In a February 1908 article in *Country Life,* Travis modestly stated, "There was opened quite recently a new golf course which promises to be one of the best in the whole country in the very near future. It embodies several new ideas in the layout—new, at all events, to this side of the water."

Travis believed he had designed a course that would allow access to all—both in the realm of membership and playability. The course, now known as The Eisenhower Park Golf Club, was originally named Salisbury Links, and players were invited to form membership groups that could then apply for playing privileges, allowing a wider range of the golfing public to use the new facility.

The design was also planned to accommodate all levels of players, from the duffer to the crack, and the success of their games was dependent on playing from the correct set of tees and choosing the paths that their abilities allowed them to successfully negotiate. His description of the fifth hole was indicative of his vision: "The fifth is 352 yards. The tee shot for the hole involves a carry of 145 yards. An intervening road runs diagonally across. While a straight shot, direct on the hole, gives a very good approach, the more one bears to the right the easier the approach becomes, but the greater must the carry be from the tee; Conversly, the more one bears to the left of a direct line to the hole, the easier the carry becomes, until finally it reduces itself to one within the compass of the merest tyro. But the more one bears to the left the harder—not to say longer—the approach becomes, both by reason of the dip of the ground and also because of the presence of hazards contiguous to the green, on the left."

This tenet, the very essence of strategic design, is so common in our courses today it is hard to imagine how radical it was at the

The SALISBURY LINKS at GARDEN CITY

is a public subscription course, OPEN TO ALL GOLFERS.

Unlike most courses, it is adapted for BOTH the BEGINNER and the EXPERT, *and it is playable all the year round.*

It is owned and maintained by the Garden City Company.

Its 18 holes—FULL OF VARIETY—are 5900 yds. in length.

It is ONLY 18 MILES FROM NEW YORK and within ten minutes walk of the Railway Station and Hotel.

Its commodious club house adjoins the first tee and provides ample locker rooms, baths, lounging room, bar and luncheon-room—with separate accommodations for ladies—all the facilities, in short, of a first class club.

The professional, R. Wakerly, is a first-class instructor and has a well-equipped shop for the repair and sale of clubs, balls, etc.

Annual Subscription for men, $35.00 ; for ladies, $25.00

Other charges to players are as follows:

One day . . . .$ 1.00
One week 5.00
One month 10.00
Six months 15.00

Annual charge for locker 5.00

FOR FURTHER INFORMATION APPLY TO THE

GARDEN CITY COMPANY, Garden City, N. Y.

The Salisbury Links was the second 18-hole course Travis designed, and a magnet for public play when it opened in 1907.

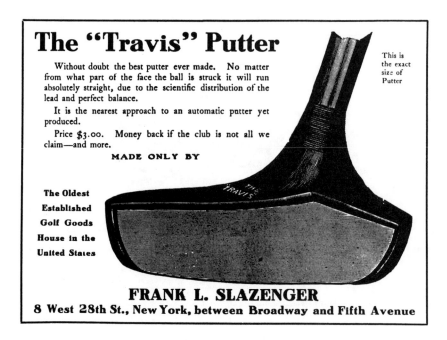
By 1907, there were many Schenectady putter copies
in the marketplace.

time. Courses were either devoid of bunkers and hazards or rife with problems from which there was little escape for any player. Travis was incorporating options and alternatives into his efforts, and he felt this tactic would be embraced by members of the upper echelons who had seen well-planned courses overseas and were aware of the absence of options here.

"In point of fact, I consider it furnishes the best test of golf that is to be found on this side—hard for the good player who is not toeing the mark practically all the time—easy for him when he is playing all his shots as they should be played—hard, extremely hard for the average player who—to use a vulgarism—essays to bite off more than he can chew; yet easy for the same player, or even one of the duffer class, provided they resign themselves, in most cases, to the loss of a stroke on the great majority of holes, by playing safe and not attempting anything beyond their known limitations—which they never will do."

Travis also protected par at the greens, something that until this time was unknown in the United States, so that even if the top player arrived there in the prescribed number of strokes, his task was yet to be completed. "Nearly all the greens are of an undulating character, some, perhaps, a little too much so." No matter what challenges certain holes offered, the majority of them in America at this time ended at flat greens devoid of movement and character.

The Old Man couldn't help but end with a swipe at the nearby Garden City Golf Club. "It is quite within the bounds of probability that the opening of the new course and the unfolding of its possibilities may suggest to the powers that be of the older club the wisdom of taking a leaf out of Salisbury's book and making additional improvements in the older course—in short, copying some of their ideas."

While Travis had been allowed to integrate some of these principles into Pinehurst in 1906 and at the Garden City Golf Club (pending the approval of the membership), the opening of Salisbury in the fall of 1907 finally afforded him an 18-hole showcase. Travis was disappointed in the quality of the turf for the inauguration, but he hoped it could become equal to his home course in subsequent seasons.

Ten years later, when J.J. Lannin, the proprietor of the Garden City Hotel wanted to open the course to all the guests of the hotel, rather than select groups who had formed clubs that held privileges, the membership balked. Rebuffed, Lannin took the large piece of property adjacent to Salisbury and installed the first of five Devereux Emmet-designed courses, all part of what would become known as Salisbury Country Club. The Salisbury Links went private, and changed the club's name to the Cherry Valley Club—and to add insult to injury, Emmet was engaged to modify the more-radical portions of the Travis layout.

In the summer of 1908, Travis had another opportunity in golf course architecture. Travis was a frequent visitor to the Essex County Golf Club in Manchester, Massachusetts, and it was there that he had met Donald Ross, resident summer pro in the months he vacated Pinehurst. During an August 1908 invitational match play event—one in which Travis would win out over 110 other entrants—Travis suggested that some changes were in order for the golf course.

The initial holes at Essex had been laid out by H.C. Leeds. Additions had been made by Willie Campbell and Ross, though Travis felt there was still room for substantial improvement. Travis brought

John Duncan Dunn with him, and the two suggested changes, most of which were implemented the following spring. The work entailed cutting into the surrounding woods to open up several of the holes, removing cross hazards from a few locations and lengthening the 13th and 14th holes, with new bunkering adjacent to the putting surfaces. Herb Wind recounts one of the famous stories about Travis at Essex that provides insight into his success as a golfer and enhances his legend.

"He and the consulting parties were discussing the probabilities of turning a stretch of land into a new short hole. Asked how far he thought it was to a certain tree, Travis estimated the distance to be between 155 and 157 yards. "Why not say between 155 and 160 yards, Walter?" someone asked. "It isn't," Travis answered. "It's between 155 and 157 yards." He hadn't meant to be dogmatic, but he had seemed so sure of his estimate that the group decided to measure the distance and see how close The Old Man actually was. He was a little off. The tree was 157 and 1/2 yards away. This incident impressed upon those to whom it was related a fact about Travis that they had always sensed but never quite known: he was an infallible judge of distance."

The changes that were made in May of 1909 on the basis of the Travis and Dunn report were very short-lived. Two years later, Ross gutted the course, leaving little intact, save the famous third green. According to all available sources, that green, originally plotted in 1893, has remained untouched for 107 years, making it the oldest green still in use in the United States.

Travis's playing talents remained sharp throughout 1908. He won the Nassau Cup in June, the Western New York golf championship in Buffalo in July (by playing cunning shots beneath a stiff wind), and the first annual amateur Poland Spring Championship in Maine in August.

In September, the fourteenth playing of the Amateur Championship was held at Garden City. Although it had been five years since Travis had triumphed in the event, many felt he was destined to win at his home club, especially considering the changes that he had made to toughen up the course. For the third consecutive year, and for the sixth time overall, Travis won the qualifying medal. This time, he was an amazing nine strokes better than his nearest competitor—Jerome Travers.

Golf was serious stuff to The Old Man.

Travis rolled through his first match, then met Henry Wilder—a young Harvard student who had won the intercollegiate title the previous fall, and was less than half Travis' age—in the second round. The youngster was exceedingly nervous on the first tee at Garden City, and when he fumbled through three putts on the first green, he lost a hole he should have won. But Travis was clearly off his game, and his problems included a rarer-than-eagle four-putt on the eighth green. When the morning play was concluded, Wilder stood four up.

The afternoon was crazy. Travis lost two early and went to six down. But on the seventh, Wilder took sick and had trouble finishing the hole. He stumbled through the next few holes and Travis took three straight to get back to two down at the 10th. But Wilder steadied himself and began winning again. By the time they reached the 14th, the young man was again four up with only five left.

"Even for so doughty a fighter as the veteran Travis it appeared that such a deficit was too much to be made up in so short a space," wrote Innis Brown. With a half at 14, Wilder was now dormie, and the buzz went up in the crowd that Travis was about to be eliminated from the tournament. Fortunately, he didn't feel that way.

Travis won the next two, but on 17 he faced a 40-foot putt for a four, while Wilder had a mere 10 feet to negotiate to end the match. The Old Man blocked out the distractions, rolled in the snake and waited for his opponent, who still could end the contest by holing his putt. When he missed they headed for 18, a hole Travis won with a par.

The match went to extra holes. After losing four straight to squander the contest, it would have been understandable for Wilder to collapse then and there. But he didn't, and after four extra holes they were still knotted. Finally, on the 41st hole of the match, Travis made a birdie three. When the young player could not duplicate the score, Travis won the longest match in USGA history to that date.

Many expected Travis to have some trouble the following morning. Instead, he easily disposed of Thomas Sherman from Yahnundasis by 8 and 7—setting up yet another confrontation between Travis and Travers that was followed by more than 1,500 spectators according to the *Times*. "They were rewarded by golf of marked brilliancy, rare steadiness, with a succession of exciting features that will make the game go down in history as one of the greatest contests ever seen in this country."

Travis led by a single hole after the morning round. However, despite heroics of every dimension, he faced an equal *deficit* after 27 holes. But he battled back and won the 10th and 11th to regain a one-hole lead. He added another hole by the time they reached the 15th tee and it seemed unlikely that Travers could overcome the difference. But then Travers won three in a row with superb play, and they came to the home green with the younger player one up on the veteran. It was there the unthinkable happened.

Travers played first and found the putting surface on the par 3 with a safe shot to the right, 15 feet from the cup. Travis knew he had to go right at the flagstick to have any chance, but his shot came up short and it fell into one of the deep, fluffy-sanded bunkers that he himself had installed to make the course tougher. After he failed to get out with two tries, Travis picked up his ball and congratulated the winner. It was an ironic end to his chance at victory, and many people thought that he would never have a better opportunity to recapture the championship that he had once owned.

A New Venture

Though Travis himself was not yet ready to make that admission, he did have other things on his mind in late 1908. A writer his whole life, with a devoted audience that waited for his articles in the wide range of publications that he contributed to, Travis sought a permanent vehicle to express his opinions.

There already were two golf magazines in existence at the time. The *Golfers Magazine* was published in Chicago, starting in 1902, and was the voice of what was then known as the western region. Chick Evans served as editor for part of its life and the magazine would exist until 1931. On the East Coast, the USGA had supported various magazines since its founding. First there was *Golf* and *American Golf*, which merged with *The Golfer*, then absorbed *Golfing* and later became *Golf* magazine again. It would continue to be published until 1917, when, some say, it was forced out of the market by *The American Golfer*.

Travis felt there was room for improvement in both the magazines when he was mulling over the launch of *The American Golfer*. There was little instruction that was accompanied by photographs, and he knew that the public cried out for such, especially from the top players. An announcement calling for subscriptions that was sent to many clubs around the country promised that articles written by famous golfers "will be illustrated with snap shots and will form a basis of sound instruction far superior to anything previously published."

Along with newspaper sports writer Jason Rogers as associate editor, Travis promised "a magazine for the maintenance of the best traditions of the Royal and Ancient game, to promote its best and highest interests, to inculcate sentiment so that there may be no sectional differences, no North, no South, no East, no West, but one whole glorified union on broad, national lines, liberal, tolerant and conciliatory in tone and spirit, a brotherly band working in unison for a common end—humble, whole-souled worshippers at the shrine of Golfiana."

He promised that any questions sent by readers would be answered by the editor, that there would be descriptions of famous

The American Golfer

The American Golfer, Inc.

49 Liberty St.

circulating as it does among a select class of buyers throughout the country, offers exceptional opportunities for "quality" advertising—no deadwood. Advertising rates furnished on application.

Travis founded *The American Golfer* in 1908 and dedicated it to the highest golfing ideals, hoping the business community would recognize its quality and reward it with their advertising.

matches from home and abroad, and that each issue would contain expert instruction that would improve the reader's game. He opened with a set of articles by Jerome Travers, explaining exactly how he plays the commanding shots that have won him championships and that "Mr. Travis, who is familiar with all parts of Mr. Travers' game, will analyze it and ask a series of questions of Mr. Travers. These questions and answers are published and bring out a fund of useful information of value to all ambitious golfers."

The American Golfer promised it would be devoted to comment, instruction, and gossip regarding the game, that it would be conducted by golfers for golfers, that it would appeal to all grades of golfers from duffers to experts in every region of the country, "not forgetting the lesser—but none the less important—side lights in the way of semi-tragical and humorous experiences which are the inevitable concomitants of all lovers of the game."

Wouldn't you love to have some of those prizes today?

The magazine's offices were installed at 49 Liberty Street in New York and Travis left the brokerage house to attend to the affairs of the magazine full-time. The ambitious plan was to publish monthly in the off-season and bi-weekly from July through September. He lined up regional correspondents to cover events in as many locales as he could, and to protect them from the scrutiny of the amateur versus professional hawkers, gave them all a pseudonym. It was "Lochinvar" covering the Western region. "Bunker Hill" handled New England. "Hazard" held court around Philadelphia. "Buckeye" reported from Ohio. Both "The Judge" and "The Colonel" issued reports from the South. "Far & Sure" was in Eastern Pennsylvania; "William Pitt" was in the Western part. "Argonaut" detailed the Pacific news, and "A Sufferer," "The Duffer," "The Philosopher," and "Westward Ho!" all submitted to the magazine from time to time. The identities of some of the correspondents and columnists remain a mystery yet today, prompting some to speculate that whenever it suited his fancy, Travis took on another name and let the doctrine fly.

The magazine was 6 and 3/4 inches by 10 inches, not the oversized 9 and 3/4 inches by 12 and 3/4 inches *American Golfer* that is commonly seen by golf collectors. The larger size was instituted many years later when Travis stepped down as editor. The covers featured an elaborate frame, New York and the date up top, an orange center color field with simply *The American Golfer* and Walter J. Travis, Editor written on it. Subscriptions were $3 a year when a day's golfing at one of the nicer resorts cost $1. Initial response was modest but encouraging, and the investors that Travis had lined up to support the project were pleased. Those investors included Walter Harban of Washington, DC, David Forgan of Chicago, Leonard Tufts of Boston, Archer Wheeler of Fairfield, Harrison Caner of Philadelphia, H.C. Frick of New York, and a host of other captains of industry and men of means throughout the country. A new phase of The Old Man's wondrous career was underway.

The Monthly Gospel

With the debut of *The American Golfer* in November 1908, Travis now had a soapbox from which to pontificate, and pontificate he did. The first issue contained a variety of articles, more photographs than had ever appeared in *Golf* magazine, several clever drawings, a few ads, some short poems, and plenty of Walter's personality.

There was a suggestion regarding simplifying the scorecard and how handicaps were posted on it. It was touted as "a method for doing away with the necessity of turning over the score card to ascertain on which holes strokes should be taken." The common organization of the information at the time was in a linear chart where, for example, if you were a 12 handicap, you looked down the list on the left, found 12, looked across the line and learned that you received strokes on holes 1, 2, 3, 4, 6, 7, 8, 10, 13, 15, 17, and 18. Travis's suggestion was to indicate a single number next to the hole number, as we know it today. This method is now universal, but at the time of the unveiling, he asked any club that adopted the system to let him know.

A section titled "Around the 19th Hole" had news and notes from around the metropolitan area primarily, but reached outward to any section of the country from which news could be gleaned. He quoted *Golf* on a matter close to his heart—the changes at Garden City. "It is true that mistakes have been made at Garden City and theories have been carried to an extreme..." wrote the competition. The passage that was quoted went on to present a case for the absurdity of the bunkers fronting the 18th green.

Travis countered: "Is the writer of this expert [?] criticism aware of the fact that the bunkers in question are an exact duplicate of those at the 11th hole at St. Andrews (Scotland) with the exception that the smaller one, on the right, is nearly a foot shallower and the one on the left fully a foot shallower than the originals? In every other respect, however, they are replicas of their prototypes. It is sufficient to add that the 11th at St. Andrews is conceded to be one of the very finest short holes in the world."

There was a brief dissertation on a common error in golf terminology. "What, for instance, is more common than 'Greens Committee' or 'Four-ball foursomes'? Both are wrong. They are sole-cisms," Travis instructed. "The committee in charge of a course is a 'Green Committee.' The whole course, or links, is a green, a term in general use in Scotland in the early days, but by some strange corruption of ideas, with an eye only to the putting greens and not to the green as a whole, the uninformed writers on this side jumped to the conclusion that the proper designation was that which has erroneously continued in current use these many years." Despite Walter's admonition, this strange corruption—and the corresponding error of calling the greenkeeper a greenskeeper—still exists today, even among some of the more informed sportswriters.

The Eastern Department featured New England Notes by "Bunker Hill." The correspondent also covered intercollegiate matches, the Lesley Cup, the Boston women golfers who played in the amateur championship at the Chevy Chase Club, and changes to Boston area courses. "Bunker" noted that "The three new holes at The Country Club—very fine ones indeed—will be ready next fall."

In "Hints and Suggestions," it was noted that "The Editor will be glad to suggest to subscribers certain methods of correcting slicing, pulling, etc. To assist in getting to the seat of the trouble, it is recommended that the stance, grip and swing be described clearly and concisely, accompanied, if possible, with photos taken in action." The suggestions included in the first issue were brief but timely: "Too little attention is paid to the oiling of shafts in fine weather and too much in wet. Never oil shafts unless they are thoroughly dry; oiling when they are wet helps to keep the dampness in." There was also this perplexing bit of instruction: "If you are troubled (happy mortal if you're not!) with jumping your head up too soon after a shot, commonly called 'taking your eye off the ball,' try putting your right foot *on the spot where the ball was* after you have struck it."

A section marked "Foreign Notes" indicated that one of the leading writers of the United Kingdom was to be the special correspondent, with reports beginning in the December issue of matches and current events. The editor also planned to educate the public about the courses in Great Britain, which they had barely heard about, and rarely seen—information of this type was uncommon in the first decade of the 1900s. "It is purposed to give a graphic description of each of the various championship courses in England and Scotland, supplemented by illustrations. The whole subject will be treated in a manner differently to anything ever attempted before."

The inaugural issue also included the first article in the series by Jerome Travers on his golfing technique, a small section of Correspondence—with one strange letter from Chicago that said, "Please do not invade my retreat with a copy of *The American Golfer,* but let me wish you success with my golf-mad countrymen," and a section on the new rules put forth by the USGA.

Travis had always been a strict adherent to the rules, at a time when their validity was still being debated and the number of people who understood them was rather small. Travis was considered a rules specialist, and just one month after the launch of *The American Golfer, The New York Times* identified him as editor of the new magazine and as a man who "has made as close a study of the technicalities of golf as anyone in this country." He believed in teaching the rules to all golfers and he attempted to explain the new codes in his magazine, and for the December 6, 1908 edition of the *Times.* "The new rules, as a whole, will be hailed with delight and universal approval by all loyal supporters and true lovers of the royal and ancient game," Travis wrote.

One rule appeared to emanate from a dispute Travis experienced at the 1904 British Amateur when he accused his opponent of grounding his club in a bunker, but the player claimed the tuft of grass his ball perched on in the sand was not part of the hazard. The new rule stated clearly that a ball is considered in a hazard whether it is on grass or not, which meant that under no circumstances could the club be grounded. Naturally, Travis applauded that.

He detailed new rulings that allowed brushing aside worm casts, snow, ice, and other loose impediments with the golf club, and that it was no longer necessary to "drop a ball from the head." Instead one must "face the hole, stand erect, and drop behind, over the shoulder." He noted that practice swings were not allowed anywhere on the course, except the tee, and he discussed stymies.

Travis was not a fan of stymies, though the laying of stymies and the techniques of jumping them was a sanctioned part of the game in his era. In nonchampionship events, if both parties agreed, matches could be played without stymies—until the rulings handed down in 1908. Despite his personal disagreement, Travis adhered to the party line and even tried to find a defense for their inclusion.

"Stymies form an integral part of the code, and, therefore, should be played. They are defensible on the ground that they are capable of being negotiated by the exercise of the highest degree of skill. In match play competition it is absolutely essential that all contestants should be compelled to play stymies, otherwise great injustice may be worked. The new rules make their playing compulsory under penalty of disqualification."

A Third Met Championship

In 1909, Travis was 47 years old. He was producing an enormous output of writing, had his hands full with a new business, and still managed to remain competitive on the amateur circuit. He won his third Metropolitan amateur championship in addition to several other tournaments. Among them was the Western New York Golf Championship played in Buffalo in July, where he defeated W.M. Reckle of Toronto 7 up with 5 to play, breaking the amateur course record with a 70. He also won at Atlantic City in May. The *Times* noted, "Playing with characteristic indifference, Walter J. Travis of Garden City won the chief cup through a downpour of rain." To do so he beat H.B. Heyburn, a University of Pennsylvania freshman—nearly 30 years his junior.

The fifteenth U.S. Amateur was held at the Chicago Golf Club in September and Travis was not up to snuff during the qualifying, bringing in 163 against Chick Evans's 151. He faced fellow Ekwanok member Fred Herreshoff in the first round and the close battle was decided in Travis's favor on the 19th green. He then ousted W.C. Fownes—who had twice performed that act on him—in the second round by 4 and 3. But Travis was blindsided by eventual champion Robert Gardner in the semis.

Throughout the year *The American Golfer* lived up to its editorial promise. Month after month Travis wrote comprehensively on a wide range of issues. In March and April he tackled "The Care of Golf Courses" and many of the solutions and suggestions he offered would be sound advice today. This was before Piper and Oakley had published their seminal work *Turf for Golf Courses*, and before any organized research effort was underway, either through the USGA, the federal government, or state universities.

Travis advocated seeding a green rather than sodding: "Turf, no matter how good, is never the same when transplanted from its natural habitat." Despite his preference for seeding, Travis went on to explain the correct way to sod a green if you must do so, and a crew following the advice today would produce a world-class surface.

"All greens should be cut and rolled every day during the growing season. And the closer they are cut the better. It is impossible to

Practicing for hours in typical get-up.

get a really fine green otherwise. If the cutting is done north and south today, tomorrow it should be east and west, and so on alternately," he wrote. He had advice on how to kill weeds and said he watched it practiced on thousands of weeds at Garden City without failure. And he believed in sanding the greens.

"The use of fine, sharp, white sand (sea sand) helps considerably in making grass finer. Or inland sand, if fine, answers almost as well. Apply during the winter—never in warm weather. The trouble

with the vast majority of greens in this country is that the grass is
too coarse. The only remedy is to impoverish the soil by the yearly
and liberal use of sand, helped along also by constant cutting and
rolling." He found little reason to fertilize greens unless there was
an extreme poverty of the soil.

The following month he laid out "The Constituents of a Good
Course," with a liberal plug for his friend Charles Blair Macdonald's
soon-to-be-opened National Golf Links and its slightly undulating
surface, neither flat nor hilly. "Anyone who has seen Prestwick, or
Sandwich, St. Andrews or dozens of other natural golf courses in
Great Britain will readily recognize the ideal. Sad to say, we have
nothing like it on this side—that I know of! The nearest approach to
the real thing is the National Golf Links at Shinnecock Hills, just
nearing completion."

Travis saw the National, Salisbury Links, and his refinements to
Garden City as the new wave of American golf. "We are on the dawn
of a new era, and a great responsibility rests on those who would
essay course architecture, whether in the making of new courses, or
the changing of old ones."

He lectured on golf ethics in June; talked about sportsmanship,
how to be a good loser—since you're bound to lose more than you
win—and how a man's best and worst traits are "luminously brought
forth and exposed to view in all their nakedness."

A few months later, however, he couldn't resist a little dig at the
British, even though it was carefully hidden in an instruction article.
Travis maintained that the slow takeaway that was preached at the
turn of the century was no longer relevant. The difference in the
rubber core ball to the feathery, and the stiffer, rather than whippy,
wood shafts, were mitigating factors to the slow backswing. He cited
the fact that all the crack players go back as fast as possible.

The reason this was not being translated to the average player,
Travis postulated, was because it was being taught by an old-fash-
ioned Britisher. "Regard for orthodoxical, traditional observances is
a sort of religion with him...inherent, the result of countless years of
narrow training, bound down by slavish imitation, to the point even
of rank conservatism." Grudge? What grudge?

To really sum it up, he said: "Even to this day, if the average
Britisher goes off his game, temporarily, what does he do? Does he
make any serious attempt to discover the underlying cause? Not a

bit of it. He simply lays off...and waits for his game to come back. We have yet scarcely emerged from our swaddling clothes, but we have a clearer perception of the laws of cause and effect. And we keep at it...until we think we have found the source of the trouble."

Playing with Presidents

During this summer Travis became acquainted with U.S. President William Howard Taft, an avid golfer and admirer of amateur competition. They played together for the first time in June 1909—the introduction coming through Vice-President J.S. Sherman who hailed from the Utica, New York area and whose son was having success in the tournament ranks. In a letter of May 31, 1909, the vice president confirmed a golf day with Taft on June 12 and suggested Travis stay with Sherman at the Albany Hotel while in Washington.

An article shortly after was headlined "Not Bumble-Puppy: Taft Wins Praise from Travis for Golfing Skill." The match pitted Travis and Taft against Col. Clarence Edwards, chief of the bureau of investigation and Captain Archibald Butt, military aide to the President, the former giving the latter two strokes a hole on the inward nine and still winning 1 up. "President Taft plays an excellent game of golf for a man his size and training," said *The New York Sun.* "In playing yesterday the President demonstrated that he is far above the novice class and is a full-fledged graduate from the bumble-puppy class to which he has heretofore claimed he belonged. Former champion Travis complemented Mr. Taft on his free and natural style." Taft often scored in the mid-90s on the Chevy Chase Club course.

In September of 1910, Travis contributed a long dissertation on golfing with the President to the *Century Magazine.* It started by reciting Taft's 15- year love of golf and how his ascendancy to the White House has given many men the courage to take up golf. "Until golf was introduced here," Travis wrote, "there was little in the way of outdoor sports to appeal to the man who had reached, to say nothing of having passed, the prime of life. Now all this is changed, and Mr. Taft has been a potent factor in bringing it about."

There was more. "Many a man I have met who have freely and gratefully admitted that golf has saved his life. Mr. Taft has, both by example and precept, directly been the agency which has given numberless men a new lease on life."

But why stop there? "A round of golf, even though it be indulged in only once a week, puts a man in better shape for his daily task, no

152

matter what his profession or occupation. Golf makes better hus-
bands, better citizens, enriching both the domestic and civic circles."

The account of their match, which followed in minute detail,
could only be a letdown after the striking prose that preceded it.
Travis also had a few gems on Taft's golfing skills. "The President
does play a good game—a very good one considering, if I may be
allowed to say so, the handicap of avoirdupois." Spoken like a true
politician—during his presidency Taft tipped the scales around 325
pounds, and at one point he had grown so large that he got stuck in
the White House bathtub.

And finally: "I know personally scores and scores of golfers who
would almost be tempted to sell their immortal souls could they but
put up such a game as he does." Was he looking for a cabinet ap-
pointment?

In November, *The American Golfer* ran a portion of a speech delivered by Taft in California in October. He extolled the virtues of
walking while playing golf by saying, "Golf is a game that leads you
to walk without realizing that you are walking." He also expressed
his hopes that the game would grow in the public sector as it has in
Scotland, and glowed over the fact that golf was a game one could
play in their senior years. "Indeed, I have played with a gentleman
very close to 80, and he beat me."

With all the flowery words, Taft made one excellent point: "It is
a game full of moments of self-abasement, with only a few moments
of self-exaltation, and we Americans, who are not celebrated for our
modesty, may find such a game excellent training."

It was during his association with Taft that Travis visited the
Chevy Chase Club. In the spring, in conjunction with Donald Ross,
Travis walked the course and offered suggestions and sketches for
improvements to green sites. They also discussed the irrigation of
the course, which was installed during the summer while the other
architectural work was being performed. By the fall, the new course
was completed and back in play.

When the Metropolitan Golf Association published its annual
handicap list in April, Travis was the only player of the 500 who
was listed at scratch. The previous year he had shared that honor
with Travers, but now Travers had joined Herreshoff at one, while
Findlay Douglas and Princeton champion Albert Seckel were listed
as two.

Travis posted another year of competitive successes in 1910. At the beginning of April, he won the North and South Amateur at Pinehurst for a second time, defeating W.R. Tuckerman 5 and 4 with some magnificent putting. Upon his return to the metropolitan area in late April he beat Fred Herreshoff for the chief cup at the Lakewood tournament, squaring accounts after the opposite result the previous year.

In May, he outlasted Travers in the Garden City Invitational one up. After being one down in the morning match, he started the afternoon with three straight 3s to propel himself back into the lead. Though Travis was thought of as a short hitter, the *Times* did note the following illustration of the strength of the wind, and the length Travis had added to his game with improvements in technique and technology since his start in the late 1800s. They were playing the 500-yard fourth hole with the wind at their backs. "Both drove nearly 300 yards, and Travers on his second shot went clear over the green."

Entering the Metropolitan, Travis was undefeated for the season, having captured the trophy in every event in which he enrolled. His run came to an end in the second round of the Met, played at the Morris County links, at the hands of C.H. Brown on the 22nd hole.

He bounced back at Apawamis a month later, winning both the medal and the matches. Expected to face Travers in yet another confrontation, Travis instead beat W.R. Thurston. Thurston was scheduled to play Travers in a semifinal contest, but Travers failed to show up at Apawamis for the match.

Travis was only four strokes shy of Herreshoff's medalist number at the 1910 U.S. Amateur, played at The Country Club. But he only won one match in Brookline, falling to a sound drubbing by John Anderson of Woodland, 5 and 3 in the second round. His failure to put on a charge at another Amateur was frustrating, and Travis was beginning to realize that despite all his success, the Amateur trophy might never be his again.

Before the season ended, however, he added wins at four more stops. At the Tuxedo Club in September, where the *Times* referred to him as the "Garden City wizard," he set the course record. "After the first few holes of the afternoon it was apparent to all that Travis was in one of his low-scoring veins. Playing par golf at almost every hole, the veteran reached the turn in 33. He came back in 36 and beat Douglas by a 4 and 3 margin. The 69 is a new record for the links."

In October it was Nassau, where he shot 72 in the final and beat John Ward 3 and 2. Then it was Atlantic City, where he met little opposition for another triumph. In November, he finished the season by capturing the Lakewood Invitation at the expense of George Brokaw. For the season, Travis had entered 10 events and won 8. While the two biggest prizes had escaped his grasp, it was a remarkable year for anyone—much less a 48-year-old among the college students.

Stirring Up the Hornets

Despite the fact that six years had passed since his win at Sandwich, Travis still managed to stir up the hornet's nest of British sentiment with an article in the March issue of *The American Golfer* about his 1904 win. Some might have taken offense to his drinking claims. "The only training I went in for was drinking, for me, huge quantities of stout—stuff you can drink in that cold, damp climate at that time of year with impunity...and most anything else alcoholic for that matter...but which on this side would be almost suicidal."

Some might also have bristled when he talked about his training regimen at the hands of the board of strategy. "Listening nightly to Sim Ford descant glowingly...yet with that characteristic gloomy sort of look at me through the corner of his eye, commingled with a grave pity that my end was soon to come...on the magnificent golf which he had seen that day played by Maxwell, Ball, Laidlay, Hutchinson, Blackwell, or one or the other of the big guns. All of which, I shrewdly suspect Ford knew and accordingly kept on pumping such stuff into me, made me inwardly resolve to grit my teeth and win the next day's matches. 'Twas the best kind of training I could have had. I was never allowed to forget for a moment that I was 'up against it.'"

Still others may have scoffed at his excuse for turning down the British offer a week later to attend a dinner in commemoration of his win. "I am extremely sorry, gentlemen, but I cannot accept your very kind invitation for the simple reason that Mrs. Travis has arranged to go up to London tomorrow morning and it was understood that before the tournament everything was made to be subservient to golf, but after the tournament I was to become her slave."

Or perhaps the biggest insult of all was what he said about the putter that so many had flocked to buy after the tournament. "The singular thing about that Schenectady which I used throughout the championship is that I have never been able to do anything with it since. I have tried it repeatedly but it seems to have lost all its virtue." Twisting the screw, perhaps?

Travis's admissions brought angered responses from the British press. Writing in the *Sporting and Country House Supplement*, "The

Caddie" said: "Just at the moment the golfing public are distinctly displeased with you as the revelations you have recently published in connection with your visit to these shores in 1904, when you had the effrontery to run away with our championship at Sandwich, are not at all pleasing reading, and in the opinion of everyone who has the welfare of the game at heart it would have been better had you still kept a safeguard over those terrible secrets which you have kept locked up in your bosom for so many years."

That was merely the opening salvo in a lengthy scolding of the Old Man. "Had you given vent to your opinions within a reasonable time of your return to your adopted country there might have been some excuse, but to nurse them for so long and then hurl them defiantly forth savours of a species of cold-blooded venomous spite which I trust I may be forgiven for saying is an act not quite in keeping with the spirit of a true sportsman."

"The Caddie" admitted that Travis was right in his squabble over the grounding of a club by his opponent, but that he had approached it poorly; that Travis played the best golf of anyone that week, but the majority of his opponents were off their game when they played him; that Travis was scorned by officials, but only because he made it clear he wanted to be left alone; and that while his success was not popular, it was merely because of his own personality. He even dragged out the incident where Travis's less-than-brilliant caddie picked up his ball, and only through a show of sportsmanship did his opponent not claim the hole. "People could not help remarking, 'Would the American have been so generous?'"

Perhaps it was pure coincidence, but in May the Royal and Ancient voted to ban all mallet-type putters based on questions put forth by other clubs, seemingly unrelated to Travis and the Schenectady.

Even the respected *New York Times* wrote: "The mallet putter, and in fact many of the freak clubs which have come into the game of golf during the past few years, and which tend to make radical departures from the old style, are for the most part American innovations, and the action by the Rules of Golf Committee is taken by some as a direct slap at the golfers on this side of the water."

Details regarding the history, development, and fate of the Schenectady are covered elsewhere in this book. But suffice it to say that when the ruling was made public on May 9, 1910, it was not a

" It's good enough for me! "

When the Royal and Ancient banned the center-shafted putter, and the
USGA did not, American cartoonists offered this sentiment
(Courtesy of Mel Lucas).

popular one in the United States or even in Great Britain, where many had taken up the instrument after Travis's showing.

Robert Watson, secretary of the USGA, for whom Travis had ordered a putter upon his return from Sandwich, issued a statement on May 20, expressing his regret for the R&A's action and consoling American golfers that the matter would soon come before the USGA and he expected a result contrary to the British ruling. "There is little likelihood that action of the same nature would be taken against the mallet putter in this country," noted Watson.

Even Travis's buddy, William Howard Taft, got into the act after Travis wrote him a long and detailed letter regarding the history of the putter. Taft wrote a short note back: "I think the restriction imposed by St. Andrews is too narrow. I think putting with a Schenectady putter is sportsmanlike, and gives no undue advantage." Whether Taft's opinion had any effect on the USGA is moot, but it did mark the first time that a sitting president publicly declared himself against an official ruling by a governing body of golf.

Throughout 1910, Travis continued to write about issues that would become part of the game's dialogue for decades to come— issues that others either hadn't thought about or were afraid to venture opinions on. He foresaw a serious problem that would affect many of the original clubs around which golf had been founded in the United States: "A very interesting problem to golf clubs adjacent to the large centers of population is presented by increasing land values. In most cases the advance has been so pronounced that the land occupied as golf courses has become too valuable for the purpose."

When clubs were set up in the midst of some cities in the late 1890s, the populations were low and land was plentiful. Subsequent growth and expansion slowly pushed development right to the club's border, and soon clubs that had once enjoyed a buffer of greenery on their periphery were abutting busy roads and buildings. Many times the roads that were mere horse paths when clubs were founded, now supported vehicular traffic that was increasing at an alarming rate. There was intense pressure for these clubs to sell their property and move to fresh fields, and, in fact, some clubs merely leased the land they used in an effort to minimize their expenses and complications if the game lost its popularity and the club was abandoned—a legitimate fear when many railed that golf was a passing fad, soon to die out in notoriety.

Travis drew on the experience of the club he knew so well. "Several valuable lessons may be learned from the experience of the Garden City Golf Club. Four or five years ago the club had an opportunity of purchasing their links for about one-third of its present value. No action was taken as the lease had then some nine years to run and the trend of sentiment among the older members of the controlling powers was, unfortunately, influenced by the fact that the unexpired term would last through their own golfing days...and that posterity would have to take care of itself when the time arrived."

Travis suggested that all clubs "make every effort to not only own their courses but to acquire sufficient additional land which may subsequently be disposed of at an inevitable enhanced value...and thus go a long way toward offsetting the original cost. The history of all golf clubs shows a substantial enhancement in value of adjacent property."

The foresight of such positions is why Travis was regarded as one of the clearest, most astute and visionary voices in American golf at the time— a position he enjoyed, cultivated, and protected.

Interested in Architecture

The breakneck pace and fully laden schedule that Travis maintained in 1910 took its toll. In the spring of 1911, he fell ill and required weeks of recuperation, a good portion of which he took at the Equinox House in Vermont. As he regained his strength, he could be found on the Ekwanok links getting his game and his stamina back. Some reports indicated that he had fallen prey to a malarial fever. But in any event, it was a wake-up call for a frail man approaching 50 years of age who had enjoyed large black cigars and unregulated alcoholic indulgence his entire adult life. A bronchial condition that had dogged him for a number of years also worsened, and though Travis never complained publicly, there were times of the year when drawing a breath was not as easy as it should be.

To maintain his writing obligations, Travis filled the magazine with updates of articles he had written in the past, while continually expanding the contributions by other writers and champions. He revisited the construction of putting greens, adding whatever insight he had gleaned since his last essay. He instructed in the techniques of putting and issued a long refutation of the banning of the Schenectady. He continued to address the issue of how to bunker a course and to deflect the criticism that never went away at Garden City.

While Donald Ross could understand the point Travis was trying to make—installing hazards that snared the better player, while allowing the foozler to innocently go about his business—there were few other golf course designers at the time that grasped the concept. Tom Bendelow was still the most prolific architect of the day and his bunker style—even when exhibited on a course that Bendelow took some time with—still left much to be desired. Many courses up until this point were created by green committees with little or no experience in the matter. A.W. Tillinghast in the East and George Thomas in the West were novices who were just beginning to dabble in course architecture and it would be years until they made their mark. Willie Park Jr., who had performed a small amount of course design in this country during brief visits in 1895 and 1909, still plied his trade in the British Isles, not setting up residence and business in America until 1916.

The better architectural efforts at the time were coming from amateur golfers who had seen golf course design in the British Isles and returned home to create one course that utilized the information they had gathered. Men like Hugh Wilson at Merion, William Fownes at Oakmont, and George Crump at Pine Valley were crafting their new courses carefully, and for a select group of individuals to enjoy. Meanwhile Charles Blair Macdonald and Dev Emmet slowly took on additional work, but the output of both was low and the demand high.

Travis knew his playing career could not go on forever, and the magazine he loved dearly was at times frustrating and worrisome, hampered by a subscription base that was not growing as it should be. Travis saw a need, as well as felt a calling, to design more golf courses. In 1911, he began to reach out.

Travis was contacted by the Youngstown Country Club in Ohio to inspect a new site they had found and hoped to move to. The club had been founded in 1898, but twice had been forced to move their nine-hole course further from the center of town. Bert Way, a transplanted Englishman from a golfing family, had planned the original course so Travis felt the members would know good golf when they played it.

Despite the fact that most of Travis's courses have been remodeled over time, one aspect of the courses that few architects have ever touched is the routing. Right from the start Travis had a feel for the flow of a course, and he demonstrated it at Youngstown. Holes vary by length, width, and direction, and there is no monotony. The course opened in 1911, and it benefited tremendously by the hiring of greenkeeper John Morley two years later.

Morley was a founding member of the Golf Course Superintendents Association of America and served for six years as its first president. He established a turf farm on the property and kept notebooks full of observations. His knowledge of course management was sought by greenkeepers throughout the country and some of his thoughts were published by *The American Golfer*. Morley oversaw a remodeling by Ross in 1921, and then hosted the 25th playing of the Western Open in 1925. Geoffrey Cornish has consulted at Youngstown in the modern era, and the Club celebrated its centennial in 1998.

Travis made his earliest exit ever from the U.S. Amateur in 1911, in part because his game was not up to its usual standards, but mainly due to the draw. He faced Travers in the first round and was beaten 3 and 2. In fact, after entering 10 tournaments in 1910 and winning 8 of them, Travis won only a single event in 1911—the Atlantic City Invitational in November. There he beat George Crump in the semi and finished McLeod Thomson 4 up with 3 to play in the final.

The British invader Harold Hilton won that amateur at Apawamis, and when he returned to England he had a joyful time criticizing the American players. In part he said: "Taking an American team of ten amateurs, what chance would they have against a team of ten British players? I will make it up as follows: Walter Travis, Frederick Herreshoff, Jerome Travers, Chick Evans, W. Fownes Jr., Oswald Kirkby, Paul Hunter, Albert Seckel, E.M. Byers, and R.A. Gardner—I think even my American friends would grant that this team would be fairly representative of American golf. Now, at least two of this team—Travis and Travers—are admittedly not quite so good as they once were, and it is possible that at one time in their career they were almost, if not quite, as good as the very best British talent, but taking the whole team on their present form, they have no men on the average of play who, to my mind, are quite the equals of one or two of our players." Hilton obviously had blocked out the drubbing he took at Travis's hands in 1904.

Travis began 1912 in Florida, seeking to regain both his health and his golf game. A little relaxation and a little practice seemed to do the trick, especially at the South Florida Golf Championship in Palm Beach in the middle of February. In the semifinal round, playing against R.H. McElwee of Onwentsia, Travis put it all together. As the match came home, spectators were amazed to see McElwee the loser 5 and 3, despite having shot a 69 on a course where 68 had stood as the course record for several years. Travis had fired a 62.

In posting a 30 on the outward half, Travis had made one 2, four 3s and four 4s. He made his only 5 on the 12th hole, but surrounded it with five 3s and three 4s, totaling 32 on the inward. It was the lowest round anyone could remember and quite a crowd had gathered to congratulate the man who had crafted it.

In the final, Travis had two 66s and brushed aside his opponent—the 1911 Florida state champion, J.R. Hyde—by a lopsided 7 and 6 margin. Travis had been brilliant from tee to green, but the famous Schenectady putter had done most of the damage, draining putts from nearly any distance after coming out from several years of retirement. *The New York Times* gave one clue as to Travis's motivation: "The championship gives Travis the first leg on a silver trophy offered by C.H. Geist, President of the Whitemarch Golf Club, and which must be won three times."

Had they given the cup for three wins in the North and South at Pinehurst, Travis would have taken it home in early 1912. Stopping in the sand hills on his way back north, Travis marched through the competition, concluding with a 6 and 5 victory over Henry J. Topping.

There were other competitive successes in the summer of 1912, including a win of the Taconic Cup at Ekwanok in July by virtue of defeating C.H. Gardner 5 and 3 in a 36-hole final, and smaller wins at Atlantic City, Rochester, and Lakewood. But by the end of the season, when *The New York Times* rated the amateurs, Jerome Travers was at the top of the list and Chicago star Chick Evans was second.

Of Travis they wrote: "Although deposed from the head of the list for several seasons, the name of Walter J. Travis, whose string of successes is, perhaps, longer than that of any other American, must be placed near the top. While it has been some time since Travis has won an important championship, he has captured several chief cups this season. As this is on a par with the success of the last two or three years, Travis is entitled to third honor."

Travis continued to speak out and inform in the pages of *The American Golfer*. In September he lobbied against the stymie, an institution he had always considered inconsistent with the ways of good golf. "It is a matter of regret that no proposal has been put forward with reference to the stymie. We should like to see the rule changed, doing away with the stymie. Some time, it may be years hence, the absurdity and injustice of the present rule in regard to stymies will be recognized by the 'powers that be.' And when that happy time arrives, as arrive it assuredly will, golfers will never cease to wonder why the old rule was permitted to remain unchanged so long. We have discussed the matter with hundreds of players at one time or another, and to our suggestion that the rule should be amended as above, we are frank to say we have not found a single dissension. The laying of a stymie is, in practically every case, a piece of unadulterated luck; it is not born of skill; and over and again it robs one's opponent of something he is entitled to as the result of skill on his part—which is not in consonance with the true spirit of the game. We have never heard any valid argument in its favor."

In the same issue, Travis introduced Henry Leach, one of England's finest writers, as a new contributor to the magazine. Leach would cover the tournaments overseas, as well as offer his impressions of American golf. Leach and Travis were friends, and both were enamored of Vermont, where they would often meet over the next 15 years to sit before a fire with others and discuss golf over a glass of whiskey and a fine cigar.

National Golf Farm Needed

Still seeking to fill a void of information about maintaining and improving the golfing grounds, Travis added a column on soil deterioration in the December issue. He pointed out that while some clubs fed their greens, few paid much attention to the soil quality of the fairways. When left unfertilized, slowly the quality of the grass would fall, and that "it is not until the actual danger point has been reached and the lies become so bad that there is any awakening." He took yet another swipe at his home club as illustration, claiming this had already occurred at Garden City.

Travis finally had an indication that someone was listening to his missives on course maintenance when he received a letter from Walter Harban of Washington, DC, in 1913. Harban was a dentist to several U.S. presidents, an accomplished amateur golfer, a club official at the Columbia Country Club in Maryland and an advocate for a national clearinghouse of turf related information. Travis published Harban's letter to *The American Golfer* in August, 1913, and it read in part: "The game of golf has taken strong hold in this country and in my judgment is destined to be our great national game. Why should not our golf courses grow and improve as has the game? The subject of growing grasses for golf courses is very new to us. I know of no treatises or place of training or any means of obtaining any information on the subject except from personal experiences of a very few men in this country who have largely been driven to work it out for themselves, and such information is not easily obtainable. What is sorely needed is the establishment of a National Golf Farm, where men can be trained for this service, where soils, fertilizers, and grasses of all kinds can be experimented with, and regardless of climatic and other conditions, worked out and given to the golfing world to guide so many in the better upkeep of the golf courses in this country."

Harban found a soul mate in Travis, who began his response with "We have no hesitation in saying that we are most heartily in accord with the suggestion put forward by Dr. Harban." Travis suggested that the benefits of a Golf Experimental Farm would be many, and offered his support for the project. Harban and Travis lobbied the USGA for the next seven years, until the USGA Green Section

166

was formed in 1920. It's doubtful that either of them could have foreseen the growth of the Green Section and the Golf Course Superintendents Association of America, and how their efforts would change the face of golf worldwide. Travis and Harban would collaborate further in the future.

Travis was right back into the competitive mode during 1913, starting with a unique win—a victory in the first golf tournament ever contested on Cuban soil. The Country Club of Havana was opened late in 1912, and Travis joined a field comprised mostly of Americans in the first days of March 1913. Once again Travis performed the hat trick, winning the qualifying by eight strokes, setting the course record of 76 strokes and capturing the Havana Cup match play trophy over R.A. Gray of the host club.

Travis added wins at Palm Beach (failing by only two strokes to match his record 62 shot the previous year), at Lakewood in April for their spring event, Oakland in May, the Tuxedo Club in June, and back at Lakewood in November for the annual fall tournament. While his supporters at Garden City hoped for a blast of magic at the U.S. Amateur at his home club—like the one young Francis Ouimet had provided in the U.S. Open at The Country Club—Travis could do no better than he had done in several years. He was four strokes behind medalist Chick Evans in the qualifying, and then fell to Evans in the semifinals by a score of 5 and 4.

Things were much the same in 1914. Once again Travis found early season success on the links with wins at Palm Beach in early February, and a defense of his Cuban title later in the month. He triumphed once again at Lakewood in May—a course where he had such a habit of winning that the members expected it, no matter what condition his game was in as the tournament approached. A week after Lakewood he won on his home links, beating Max Behr 6 and 4 in the Garden City Invitational.

Amateur vs. Professional Revisited

Throughout the spring, Travis found himself in the middle of a controversy with the USGA. The previous fall, realizing the British Amateur would once again be staged at Sandwich in 1914, Travis proposed taking a 'team' of American players overseas at his expense in an attempt to offer his coaching wisdom and hopefully see one of the cracks win the amateur title. This request came at a time when, once again, the question of amateur status was being batted around by the USGA, with opinions falling all over the spectrum.

The Woodland Golf Club of Massachusetts had offered to defray Francis Ouimet's expenses for the trip and the offer had been approved. But Travis's request was denied, prompting Travis to ask the USGA to define the distinction. When Travis made the correspondence between himself and the USGA public in April, he forced his friend and now USGA president, Robert Watson, to respond. Watson stated that he "did not care to discuss the matter except to say that the association has explained that it did not like to approve such an undertaking." Watson went on to add that he would write Travis a personal letter in which he "would give good and sufficient reasons."

The war raged on through the summer, fueled by the New York papers, pure amateurs throughout the country, and the USGA itself. In May, while some of the Americans were already in England for the championship, the question of whether amateur golfers who receive money for writing articles about golf could maintain their amateur status arose. The newspapers contended that Jerome Travers and Francis Ouimet, who had both written a series of instruction articles, might lose their amateur status. "No criticism has been made about any amateur reporting for newspapers or magazines, current or past or future golfing news. It is perfectly legitimate work in any branch of sport. Mr. Ouimet's employment by Wright & Ditson in no way affects his amateur standing."

One letter that was published regarding the controversy was written by A.H. Pogson, former chairman of the Metropolitan Golf Association Handicap Committee, who said: "I am inclined to believe that the present rating of an amateur golfer is right, with one exception. The rule should provide against the laying out of golf courses for money. It looks though, as if the United States Golf Association is going to get into a terrible muddle if it doesn't look out."

In July, Watson polled 45 prominent clubs for their opinions, submitting four different definitions of what constitutes an amateur, and asking local committees to side with one of the definitions. "Thus far the sentiment is overwhelmingly in favor of a stricter definition of an amateur." The three issues in question were whether one could still be an amateur and receive money for laying out or altering golf courses, writing articles explaining their technique, or after accepting traveling expenses or free room and board in order to play in tournaments or at exhibitions. Gathering information throughout 1914, it seemed that a decision was imminent.

The Last Major

Meanwhile the 1914 competitive season brought to fruition a dream Travis had entertained for nearly 15 years. The U.S. Amateur was played at Ekwanok in Vermont that September, and Travis acted as unofficial host to the players who made the trek. Travis realized that this might be his last and best chance at winning the championship one more time. It had been six years since he was last the medalist and 11 since he won the trophy. He knew every inch of Ekwanok and had been playing decent golf in the weeks leading up to the tournament. The draw looked good, too, because he wouldn't face Travers until late in the tournament.

Travis marched through his matches, and even had Travers three down after the first nine holes of their 36-hole encounter. But Travers fought back and went one up after the morning 18, and Travis could never recover. When he made a bogey on the 15th green at Ekwanok that afternoon, Travers closed him out 5 and 3, and Walter J. had played his last stroke in a national championship. He was 52 years old, had played in 17 straight championships, had won three times and had been medalist six times. It was a stellar record for someone who had taken up golf at an age when some national champions retire.

As editor, Travis continued to explore issues, techniques, and procedures that few other writers were tackling. In September 1914 he confronted the fact that some prominent golfers had called for a standardization of the golf ball—another issue that still surfaces some 85 years later. "Much has been said lately concerning the desirability of standardizing the golf ball. It is urged by some that the present ball can be driven so far as to spoil our courses, and a cry has been set up for the adoption of a standard ball which cannot possibly be propelled the same length. Virtually the same thing was said eight or nine years ago, when the Haskell came in, and doubtless the same talk was heard 50 years ago when the guttie was first introduced. Time has conclusively shown the fallacy of these arguments."

Travis rolled into the new year with three more wins—first at the Nassau Country Club in October, and then at Palm Beach and Lake Worth in Florida during February of 1915. But the publicity he

A rare photo of Travis laughing. This one is signed to James Taylor,
founder of Ekwanok and a long-time friend and supporter.

Putting at Ekwanok during his last appearance in the
U.S. Amateur in 1914.

received early in the year was not of a positive variety. In a February 11, 1915 article, the *Times* reported that Travis was being sued by Virginia Blackman, one of the domestics employed in the Travis home. The $25,000 suit claimed that "on or about November 18, 1914, at Garden City, New York, while the plaintiff was employed as a servant in the family of the defendant, the latter, with force and violence, ill treated the plaintiff" and forcibly pulled her from one room to another. Travis denied all the charges and the court later dismissed the case.

On his way back from Florida, Travis stopped off at Pinehurst for the annual Spring Tournament. *The Pinehurst Outlook* couldn't believe the lasting talents of the 53-year-old. "Surely golfers may come and go, but Travis goes on forever. Straight down the alley, straight to the pin, straight for the cup, just playing his own best ball with sublime, subconscious, preoccupied concentration, all of which goes to show that temperament is the stuff that makes champions, the infinite capacity for detail which is always the surest indication of genius." The Old Man averaged 75 on the Number 2 course, against the field's average of 80, and won the cup.

As the 1915 Metropolitan Amateur at Apawamis approached, Travis was contemplating another change in his amazing career. He had been in the golfing spotlight for 17 years, and for some of that time he had been at the pinnacle of the game. He was seven years into his editorship of *The American Golfer,* and the magazine had put most of its competitors out of business, but it was still a struggle. For the past two years, the controversy regarding the definition of amateur status had been an unwanted distraction and he had put his design career on hold so as not to jeopardize his efforts on the links. With his wish granted for the Amateur to be played at Ekwanok, he had bowed out of the national championship and left the future to the younger players who had been nipping at his heels for a decade.

He started the Met with a solid 7 and 6 win over Percy Pyne, but he knew his work was just beginning. He faced Jerome Travers—his nemesis of the past 10 years and the man who had eliminated him from more championships than any other golfer—in the second round. Although Travis was one up at the turn, Travers came on strong for the back nine, and it looked like once again, Travers would prevail. But Travis fought back, took the 14th, tied 15 and 16, only to lose 17 and go to the final hole one up. Travers had one last chance standing over a 25-foot putt to win the hole and send the match to extras. When the putt slid by, Travis had prevailed by shooting a solid 75 to Traver's 76.

Although the crowd thought this gave Travis a green light toward the final, he knew he couldn't let his guard down. His opponent in the quarter-finals was Percy Platt, and Platt had beaten him just a few weeks prior at Lakewood. Travis started strong by winning three of the first eight, but Platt came back to square the match and then take the lead on the 15th. Travis won 16 and tied the next two, sending the match to extra holes, where he prevailed at the first. Next he squared off against Oswald Kirkby, the region's low-handicap leader. Travis was out in 35, took three of the first four holes coming home, and beat Kirkby by 6 and 5 to advance to the final against John G. Anderson. Anderson was a recent transplant from Massachusetts who had won that region's championship several times, and had beaten Travis when the amateur was in Brookline.

NEW YORK　　　　　　　　　　　　　　JUNE, 1915

THE AMERICAN GOLFER

THE AUTHORITATIVE ORGAN OF THE "ROYAL AND
ANCIENT" GAME

Walter J. Travis
Editor

$3.00 per year　　　　　　　**30c. per copy**

This simple cover graced *The American Golfer* for years.

Over a thousand people were on hand for the final on Saturday, June 5th. "There was great speculation as to whether or not the Garden City veteran would be able to keep pace with his athletic opponent. A thirty-six hole match to Anderson probably wouldn't be any more tiring to him than a single round to the veteran. Many believed Travis would collapse," said the *Times*.

But Travis was rested and ready, and the *Times* noted: "The match was distinctly a see-saw affair from start to finish. The leader changed as frequently as the mind of a coy maid." Travis fell behind at the start, and the difference was his putting—noticeably lacking from what it had been for the previous matches. He battled back on sheer will, only to fall behind once more, before squaring after 18 had been completed.

Travis once again soared on the front nine of the afternoon round, and by the time the golfers had played 29 holes Travis was three up—but it would not last. Anderson came back with a win on 11 after a Travis shank placed him against a stone wall from which there was no recovery. A stymie that he could not negotiate cost Travis the 13th and Anderson fought back to even by winning the 15th.

"Both missed putts on the sixteenth," reported the *Times*, "Travis throwing away his chances by missing one so ridiculously small that he laughed heartily and the gallery joined in. Evidently this is what the old man needed to put young blood in his veins."

What happened on the final hole is the stuff of legends, and rather than embellish it in any way, one turns to an article that competitor John Anderson, who was standing on the green next to Travis, wrote for *Golf Illustrated* later that year. "Four months or so ago a bronzed veteran of the links bent stolidly over a very obedient rubber-core and sent it scurrying on its way towards the hole forty feet off. When the ball had gone about ten feet the player lifted his head and watched the sphere until it had finished its unerring journey at the bottom of the hole. Then again was the Grand Old Man of American golf the holder of a championship title, through the medium of victories over some of the best and lowest handicap men in the United States."

Travis had won the Metropolitan Amateur for the fourth time, this time at the age of 53, and the timing was right for an announcement he had been contemplating for some time. Anderson continued:

The Old Man

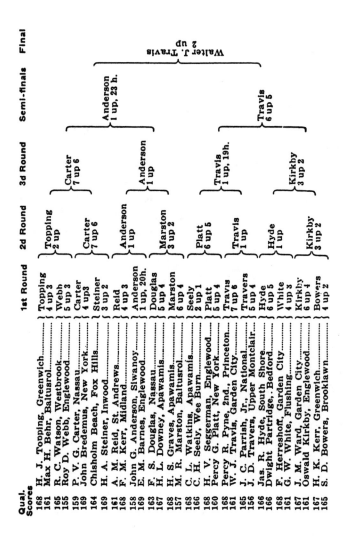

Travis marched through the field of the 1915 Metropolitan Championship, winning the title at age 53.

The classic Travis caricature
(Courtesy of Mel Lucas).

"An hour later Mr. Travis was telling his friends that he had played in his last championship battle, that the wear and tear of long struggles was too much for one of his physique, that national and sectional frays would see him hereafter as an interested spectator rather than as a golfer doing battle. I cannot imagine a finer finish to a career nor one which would be more apropos."

Travis had fought his battles with dignity, conviction, and dedication, but after nearly 19 years of it, he was done. He told his friend Henry Leach, "I am playing practically as well as ever, but I can scarcely stand the prolonged strain of a tournament lasting from three to five or six days. At the end of the third day I am pretty well 'all in.' Now it does not strike me as being quite sportsmanlike to go into a tournament in these circumstances. For the first day or two, while I am comparatively fresh, I might, if on my game, knock out one or two good men—men who might have a chance of winning ultimately. At the end of the third day almost anybody can come along and lick me."

Travis had decided in advance of Apawamis that this would be his last major tournament and that he would content himself to enter a few two-day events a year in the future. He didn't want to turn professional, but he wanted to pursue a career in golf course architecture, so the logical move was to move out of national competitions.

There were many tributes to Travis when his retirement was announced, but Anderson, the man he beat in that last Met may have said it best. "American golfers as a body must and do grant that in his withdrawal goes a man from active participation in the greatest game we have, who has ever played the game with the finest spirit of sportsmanship, the strictest personal adherence to the rules, a splendid opponent, a generous victor and a lion in defeat. No one ever heard Mr. Travis make an excuse. Did you ever think of that you golfers? Surely all of us when they gather round the festive club banquets this year should toast the past performances and the love, the passionate love, which he gives to the sport which we, too, love as best we can. Golfers may come and go but there will never be another 'Walter J.' the name by which his friends know him best."

The Architect

Turning His Attention

Dr. Harban of Columbia Country Club in Chevy Chase, Maryland, was the first to contact Travis after the word went out that he was seeking architectural work to fill the void left by his departure from championship golf. In 1911, Harban had assisted Herbert Barker with the original plan at Columbia's present location. This was after the Club had occupied two other primitive golfing grounds elsewhere in Chevy Chase.

Travis visited the site late in 1915, made suggestions to the green committee, and the work was carried out in 1916. The committee had hoped to build a course that would be second to none in America, and subsequently attract the 1920 playing of the U.S. Amateur. Travis informed them that they had fallen short, but that simple corrections could be made. With the changes, the USGA might look more favorably upon their request. Due to Travis's stature in the world of golf, club officials listened to his suggestions.

Travis's work was not major surgery and very little of it is identifiable today after subsequent remodeling by William Flynn in the 1930s and George and Tom Fazio in the modern era. Travis built some new tees, lengthened some holes, and installed a few greens with challenging slopes in them. The work was supervised by Harban and Fred McLeod, Columbia's pint-sized pro who had been hired in 1912 (he would remain with the Club until 1968!). McLeod won the U.S. Open in 1908 and was a serious contender in every major championship until 1930. He played in the first three Masters and served as honorary starter there for 15 years beginning in the 1960s. Standing just 5-foot-4-inches tall and weighing only 108 pounds, McLeod, like Travis, relied on his skill as a putter in competition. Over the years, he honed that skill by negotiating the outrageous putting surfaces Travis added at Columbia. The USGA appreciated the improvements Travis had made to the design and rewarded Columbia with the 1921 U.S. Open.

While visiting Columbia to inspect the progress in 1916, Travis collaborated with Harban on a nine-hole public course for the city of Washington, DC. West Potomac Park Municipal remains the most public course Travis ever created, and it's still enjoyed today by a

The Orchard Park Course was the first of
several designs that Travis did in the
Buffalo/Ontario area.

wide range of enthusiasts. According to Travis, he and Harban tried
an experiment on the ninth hole at Potomac: installing the "first
vegetatively planted Creeping Bent green in the country." Using plant
stolons instead of seeding the green, Travis later replanted the ninth
green at Columbia in the same manner.

In 1916, Travis was also in contact with the Park Club of Buffalo, regarding an 18-hole course they were attempting to build. The Orchard Park layout that Travis would design was the first of several contracts in the Buffalo and adjoining Ontario areas. Orchard Park has been changed several times in the 84 years since Travis was on site, first by William Harries in the 1950s, then by Dick Nugent in the 1980s, and most recently by Brian Ault in the 1990s. Ault added several holes in an old quarry, which are interesting and challenging in a modern vein, but contrary to some of the older gems on the layout. The course begins with a classic par 4 that is often repeated on similar lays of land, but never better. From an elevated tee near the pro shop, the hole falls down to a flat, wide, straight fairway, but then up again to a green set into a natural bowl with trees framing the rear and sides of the green. A stream in front of the upsweep into the green site demands a second shot of precise distance.

The second hole is one-of-a-kind par 3. Shaped like a pilsner glass, the hole emanates from a crowded tee, bordered by an embankment down to a creek on the right and railroad tracks to the left. Available land mass increased dramatically at the green, but you'd never know that, standing on the tee. Another gem can be found two holes later on a short par 4 with a heavy-lipped bunker planted squarely in the approach zone to the compact putting surface. There are few holes as memorable as the opening four until you reach the 18th, another singular golf experience with large oak trees growing from a lateral chasm in advance of the green environment. It is always hard to know, but these holes appear to be very close to their original nature, and still stand as fair golfing exams that require precise and cunning shotmaking.

Travis also completed his work for the Garden City Country Club during 1916.

Hitting His Stride

Travis's next assignment came at the Hollywood Golf Club in Deal, New Jersey. Isaac Mackie had designed an 18-hole layout on the current site, but the membership wasn't pleased. More money was spent *removing* useless bunkers that Mackie had installed than had been originally spent to construct them. Seth Raynor was at the very start of his design career in 1916, having assisted C.B. Macdonald on several projects, and he was employed to correct some of Mackie's mistakes. Still the Club was not satisfied, and despite the fact that the country was about to enter World War I, officials authorized $12,000 to have Travis put the course in championship form.

Travis was paid $1,000 in 1917 to revise the layout. He added two sets of tees on every hole, and stretched the championship tees to a previously unheard-of length of 6,950 yards. Although he retained the Mackie routing, Travis combined several holes, added two new ones, and completely reworked the greens and bunkers. The new course required length and demanded accuracy, and the members were finally satisfied after years of disgruntlement.

"The Green Committee since last fall has rearranged and improved the course, having been advised in these changes by Mr. Walter J. Travis, one of the best architects on golf course technique and construction," wrote green committee chair Frank Barrett in 1918. "The course now, with new type of greens, present distances of holes and position, and types of pits and bunkers, will prove to be one of the best and up-to-date courses in this part of the country." Barrett cited an excellent bunkering scheme, designed to challenge the better player, tees which were enlarged and turfed for increased play, hazards which will make the class player sit up and take notice and greens "no two being alike and designed to fit the length and type of hole and position of the green, and putting will never again be monotonous as heretofore." Rave reviews followed from all quarters.

"All who have played over the velvety fairways of Hollywood, or putted on the tricky but deadly accurate greens, have taken away with them a memory of one of the most perfect golf courses in the East," wrote the esteemed golf clubhouse architect Clifford

184

Travis was not afraid to use bunkering—witness the thirteenth at Hollywood Golf Club in Deal, New Jersey.

Wendehack in *Golf Illustrated* during 1929. "For, as a piece of golf architecture and beautiful landscaping, cleverly interwoven into a well balanced whole, the Hollywood Golf Course is an outstanding piece of work and a perpetual monument to the master mind who laid it out." Johnny Farrell, U.S. Open winner and long-time pro at Baltusrol, named Hollywood the second best course in the country in 1926.

Hollywood was remodeled by Dick Wilson in 1962, and then Rees Jones in 1998. Jones maintained much of the Travis feel and style, despite upgrading to modern day standards. He left the routing as it was, enhanced the bunkers by recovering their original shape and then defining them cleanly and clearly. The par-3 fourth hole, a volcanic upthrust green that is nearly smothered by wildly curving mounds and deep pit-like bunkering is a standout. Likewise the 12th— once referred to as the Heinz Hole in deference to the 57 bunkers found there—has been modernized, but its antique personality and uniqueness still shines through.

The course still receives rave reviews. Golf course architect Tom Doak wrote in his *Confidential Guide to Golf Courses*, "the detail work to the greens and bunkers is some of the neatest I've stumbled across in a long time. Travis' huge, finicky fairway bunkers are just plain neat." Head professional Mike Killian hopes that the Club will stage a USGA championship at Hollywood in the future. He certainly has the course to do it on.

Official Competitive Retirement

Although Travis continued to play in local events during 1916, his heart wasn't in it. When the USGA finally issued its ruling that prohibited course designers from competing as amateurs, Travis announced his retirement. In their decision, the USGA said that amateurs "are prohibited from accepting or holding any position as agent or employee that includes as part of its duties the handling of golf supplies, or engaging in any business wherein one's usefulness or profits arise because of skill or prominence in the game of golf."

By February 1917, Travis was done as a competitive golfer—the decision was influenced in part by his health. A note from H.C. Russell, M.D. of Palm Beach, Florida, in that issue of *The American Golfer* excused Travis from his usual editorial duties. "This is to certify that Walter J. Travis is suffering from facial Erysipelas; that he is confined to his room and is unable to do work of any kind." Erysipelas is an acute bacterial disease characterized by fever and severe skin inflammation, and Travis was out of action for the early part of 1917.

Travis worked for Canoe Brook Country Club in Summit, New Jersey, later in 1917, giving what is now the North Course a reworking that included bunker remodeling and green alteration. Subsequent work by Alfred Tull, Robert Trent Jones, Rees Jones, and the New Jersey Turnpike Authority—which rerouted the Morris Turnpike as it cuts through the course—has wiped out all but a tiny fraction of Travis's efforts. According to general manager Rudy Fisher, only the eighth hole remains true to Travis's original design.

Before Grantland Rice assumed the role of editor of *The American Golfer*, he paid homage to Travis in this 1917 cover story.

Travis worked on Canoe Brook in 1917, remodeling
the bunkers and altering the greens.

Old Guards

Travis was back in Florida early in 1918; the excursion south had become a regular part of his annual schedule. Together again with his old buddies, he played some warm weather golf and talked endlessly about the royal and ancient game. Forerunners of the Senior Tour, the veterans would play golf during the day and then retire to the porch of the Royal Poinciana or The Breakers hotels in the afternoon. Each member of the "Porch Club" had their own special chair, and as the whiskey flowed, so did the stories. Travis often recounted his British Amateur win with vigor and embellishment.

As more and more seniors were added to the clique, there was a motion made to formalize the group. Eventually, the "Old Guard Society of Palm Beach Golfers" was formed on the evening of March 7, 1918, while the group was dining aboard Walter Witherbee's yacht *Silouan*. Travis was elected the first president of the organization, with A.F. Huston as vice-president and Louis Stumer as secretary-treasurer. According to *The Palm Beach Daily News*, "The society object was agreed upon as being 'To promote the best interests of golf and good fellowship generally among golfers at Palm Beach.'" Warren G. Harding, H.B. McClellan, Walter Fairbanks, and Clarence Davies were among the charter members.

The war put architectural work on hold, as few clubs went ahead with planned renovations or new construction during the intense period when uncertainty reigned. Instead, both professional and top amateur golfers played exhibition matches for the Red Cross. Prizes, entry fees, admission charges, and auctions of golf goods from the stars were all donated to the war effort. Writer H.B. Martin helped to organize a return match between Travis and Douglas Findlay on November 10, 1918, approximately 20 years after their first famous confrontation. The contest was played at Garden City and more than 1,000 people followed the play during a strong wind that made low scoring difficult.

It is clear that the standard of play had slipped since their first meeting. Phrases such as "two indifferent shots after the drive," and "the twelfth was a comedy of errors," and "both giving a pitiable exhibition of putting," and "Mr. Travis made a hash of the tenth," were used in the report of the outcome—a one up win for The Old Man.

Sponsors had realized that the revenues derived from the matches were bolstered by auctioning off the personal belongings of the golfers and the privilege to caddie for them. There were many cases of Walter Hagen losing the fancy shirt off his back when a wealthy patron was willing to donate $25 for it. At Garden City, Martin Littleton paid $250 for the right to caddie for Travis, and a similar fee was obtained for Douglas's bag. After the play, Travis offered the Schenectady putter he had used to win the British Amateur to the auctioneer. When the gavel was finally brought down, the famous weapon had brought $1,700, the most ever paid for a golf club to that point. Lewis Lapham, a member at Garden City, bought the putter and then donated it to his golf club. Over $3,000 was raised at the auction, and nearly $12,000 was raised overall as a result of the match—the largest total of any golfing event the Red Cross sponsored.

Branching Out

Late in 1918, Travis began work on the design of two more golf courses: Onondaga Golf and Country Club in upstate New York and White Beeches Golf and Country Club in metropolitan New Jersey. Onondaga is located just outside of Syracuse, in Fayettville, and Travis made an initial inspection of the site in 1918. The club had already been in existence for 20 years at two different locations when Travis was hired to install their first 18-hole course.

Travis offered two layouts, one dependent on the club purchasing another parcel of land to the west. He believed that the additional parcel would produce a superior golf course, and the membership eventually went along with the suggestion. The conclusion of the war and a lower than normal cash flow at the club created some turmoil in financing both the new course and a new clubhouse, but the course was completed by 1921 and opened for play at 6,453 yards.

The course has been modified twice since its installation. In 1963, Hal Purdy changed holes seven, eight, and nine. Twenty years later, Sam Mitchell and Phil Wogan altered holes three and four, which stretched the course to 6,529 yards but reduced its par from 72 to 71. The course has been the site of numerous statewide championships, including the New York State Men's Amateur championship on more than one occasion.

In Haworth, New Jersey, due to the neighborhood that surrounded it, White Beeches did not have the luxury of adding more property to the parcel that Travis was given to work with. They had already merged what was originally the nine-hole Haworth Country Club with a private nine-hole course across the street that was part of New York City mayor Hugh Grant's summer estate. (Today, the roads that crisscross the property are busy, there is civilization nearby, and the club feels fortunate that their elegant green space is protected from the hustle of modern life.)

Travis planned 18 holes on the site, which was later named White Beeches in honor of the magnificent trees that shielded the course from encroachment. Though touches of Travis remain at White Beeches, and superintendent Armand LeSage has kept his memory alive, this course has been modified more than any other Travis layout. Revisions have been made by Maurice McCarthy, Alfred Tull (who designed current holes 15, 16, and 17), William Mitchell, Brian Silva, Robert McNeil, and LeSage himself. In 1999, new tees were installed on the back nine.

The opening holes clearly show Travis's influence—in their direction, fairway bunkering, and greens. The fourth is magnificent, a dogleg with massive beech trees directing your play to the right off the tee and then to the left into the uphill green. It's a treasure that has only become more valuable over time.

Travis planned two more courses before the end of the decade: the Lochmoor Club in Grosse Pointe Woods, Michigan and Westchester Country Club, where he was assisted by John S. Sweeney. Unfortunately, little of his work remains today at the private 6,796-yard Lochmoor club. The course was revamped almost immediately by H.S. Colt and C.H. Alison. It was altered again in 1960 by Larry Packard, and then again in 1981 by Arthur Hills. Today, large oak and maple trees line its fairways and clusters of bunkers protect its large, undulating greens.

Leaving His Baby

Though money had never been a problem for Travis, he was growing increasingly weary of the financial affairs of *The American Golfer*, and increasingly interested in a full-time involvement in architecture. From 1889, when he was courting Anne and making $2,600 a year (when the median wage was a seventh of that) to 1919, when he was earning around $8,000 a year (and the median was closer to his 1889 wage), Travis had never been strapped for funds. But as the 1920s loomed and he was closing in on 60 years of age, Travis felt he no longer needed the full-time writing outlet that had served him so well, especially when the finances of the magazine were an increasing problem. His wage for a year at *The American Golfer* was under $6,000, but his design fee for one 18-hole golf course was $3,000—and the demand was there.

In December of 1919, Travis entertained a takeover bid from a group of men headed by Messrs. Newton and Hawse. They were not only willing to offer a reasonable sum for the business, but also confident they could increase the circulation and the advertising revenue and get the publication back on track. The new owners wished to install Grantland Rice as editor, but keep Travis on as associate editor and director.

Travis wrote to the stockholders to sell the plan. Dividends on the preferred stock had been suspended four years previously and none had ever been issued on the common stock. "The earnings of the company have not been satisfactory in recent years," wrote Travis, "and have barely sufficed to pay the increased expenses, due to conditions created by the war." The new owners promised a one-to-one exchange for stock in the new company to the investors in the old company, with hopes of paying dividends in the near future. "We believe that the large amount of money which the investors propose and appear able to put into the enterprise will result eventually in substantially increasing the value of your property." After numerous interviews with the purchasers, and promises that the board of directors would be retained—with the addition of Rice and business manager W.J. Fawcett—Travis concluded that the deal should be approved.

I HAVE severed my connec-
tion with The American
Golfer, and will devote my
whole attention to golf course
architecture, including the laying out of new courses and
modernizing existing ones.

Then, too, for over twenty
years I have made a close study
of soils and grasses—and can
safely say there is no excuse
for poor greens or fairways
anywhere.

WALTER J. TRAVIS,
Garden City, L. I.,
New York

Travis' separation from *The American Golfer* was painful, but he
wasted no time in devoting himself to golf course design.

The stockholders agreed, and the deal was consummated. Travis
then left on an extended southern trip as he had in years past. But
things did not go exactly as planned at the magazine. Rice began to
butt heads with his new bosses, and creditors that the new owners
had promised to pay off went unpaid. By summer, Travis's relationship with Newton and Hawse had soured. On September 15, 1920,
he presented them with four conditions that had to be met for him to
continue with the magazine. They entailed a satisfaction of Hawse's
personal debt to the magazine, the allocation of stock, the curtail-
ment of undue overhead expenses, and an examination of salary
parity. When his demands went unmet, Travis resigned from *The
American Golfer*, effective October 9.

Earlier, Travis had written to his friend Henry Leach, who he
had brought into the magazine as a chief correspondent, to tell him

The khaki coat was a trademark most of his career.

of the new arrangement. On September 29, he informed Leach: "You will perhaps be a bit surprised to hear that I also have decided to sever my connection with the magazine. It's a long story, but the simple fact is I have not been treated fairly. I am rather glad, in many ways. In the future, all my attention will be given to golf course architecture, work which I love and which pays much better than magazine work."

Conditions at the magazine deteriorated rapidly after that. Rice battled with the new owners because they were not living up to any of the provisions of the sale. Rice then lined up another buyer, but the team refused to sell until it was too late and the investor had tied his money up elsewhere. Meanwhile, creditors moved in, the lease was defaulted on, and chaos reigned.

Ironically, the push that Rice had made for new subscriptions in the first months of 1920 was paying off and advertising was rebounding as well. He felt it would be a great loss for golf and an unnecessary shame for such a fine magazine to come to this unfortunate end. Consequently, Rice took the advice of Don Parker, advertising director for the Century Company—a successful publishing group known for their high-quality work—and after a meeting with president Morgan Shuster, *The American Golfer* was brought under the wing of Century starting early in 1921. Travis would contribute numerous articles to the magazine in the early years of the 1920s.

In a letter to Don Parker, thanking him for saving the magazine, Travis recounted why he left. "Realizing I had been sold, and sold cheaply, I got out...being unwilling to help along others at my own expense and resources seeing troubles ahead for the baby I had struggled so hard for, for over a decade, but which was no longer my own."

Maintaining Garden City

From his resignation at *The American Golfer* in September of 1920, until just a couple of weeks before his death in July of 1927, Travis devoted himself to golf course architecture. He would become involved with more than 25 golf courses during that time, planning many 18-hole layouts and remodeling greens and bunkers on a host of additional courses.

Late in 1920, Travis had his first contact with Charles Piper of the United States Department of Agriculture. Piper, in conjunction with Russell Oakley, had published *Turf for Golf Courses* in 1917. It was the first American book devoted to a subject that Travis had been writing about since *Practical Golf* appeared in 1901. Though its letterhead indicated that Forage Crop Investigations were their specialty, Piper and Oakley were continually inundated with turfgrass questions, and slowly they would turn their attention to the subject full-time.

Travis inquired about recent turf problems at Garden City, looking for confirmation that his beliefs about improper maintenance of the golf course were correct. Piper agreed, and suggested that the problems might be due to overfertilization, use of lime on soil that did not need it, and an absence of rolling—those very factors Travis believed had contributed to a surfeit of weeds and poor performance by the bentgrasses they were crowding out. Garden City was overseeding with Redtop, but Piper suggested that plowing up the soil to bare dirt and replanting was the only way to grow a healthy crop of new grass, as Redtop had a poor record of infiltrating existing turf and establishing itself.

In a subsequent mailing to all club members, Travis directed his observations, complaints, and suggestions to the Green Committee, a body he had given up serving on after an association that lasted from 1899 to 1911. Travis firmly believed that the course was headed sharply downhill and unless a reversal of methodology was quickly adopted the course would never return to the standard it had set in the first decade of the century.

This long-standing battle about the design, administration, and upkeep of Garden City had destroyed his friendship with Dev

Emmet—the very man who had encouraged him to enter the 1904 British Amateur and had cheered him on during his triumph. On April 21, 1921, Travis received a letter from Emmet, which simply said, "My dear Travis, We were friends so long and I have always regretted our estrangement. Cannot we be friends again? Yours sincerely, Devereux Emmet." It's unclear whether Emmet's overture ever produced the desired effect.

In October, Travis was contacted by the Cape Arundel Golf Club in Kennebunkport, Maine, a site he had visited early in the century when the club was just getting started. The members had obtained an additional 90 acres of land along the banks of the Kennebunk River and had hired Alex 'Nipper' Campbell, respected pro at The Country Club in Brookline, to lay out a new course. When Campbell failed to show as expected, the club reached out to Travis. Late in the fall, along with John Duncan Dunn, Travis made an inspection tour of the property.

Travis retained parts of five existing golf holes at Arundel and crafted the remainder from the sandy soil that presented itself in gentle waves and folds, similar to seaside links in Great Britain. "The Arundel Golf Club is no fledgling, and has been slowly expanding from a primitive nine hole links of 'huckleberry pasture' lineage to its present real up-to-date position on the golfing map," wrote the *Turn of the Tide* newspaper of Ogunquit. "The new holes as laid out by Mr. Walter J. Travis call for the finest kind of golf. They are perfectly bunkered, and the gently rolling putting greens are things of beauty, and joys forever. Mr. Travis has laid them out most scientifically, and they will call for every kind of shot that a good player is supposed to carry in his bag. Every hole, long or short, is as exactly worked out as a problem in plane geometry. To equal the par total of 69 strokes calls for perfect golf."

When he had finally finished Cape Arundel in 1923, Travis said, "While the course is on the short side it will strongly appeal to every class of golfer, from the 'crack' to the 'dub.' It looks easy, as my courses do, but the man who equals par will have played 'some' golf. Perhaps the real charm resides in the putting greens, which, 'altho I says it what shouldn't' are real beauties and will delight the soul of any real golfer."

Others have sung the praises of the greens at Arundel through the years, including former president George Bush, whose family

Cape Arundel in Kennebunk, Maine still features greens with constant movement, chocolate drops as large as a truck, and sand bunkers tight to green sites.

has made Arundel their home club while in residence at Walker Point for several generations. When asked to name his favorite golf holes by a national golf magazine a few years back, Mr. Bush started at the 13th on Cape Arundel. "At high tide, especially in the fall and spring, it is of unparalleled beauty," Bush wrote. "At low tide you see menacing flats that gobble up golf balls. At high tide you see fresh flowing salt water that makes the hole seem longer. I have many happy memories of seeing great golfers like Couples, Olazabal, Palmer and Irwin playing this hole. But also so many memories of family games. My grandfather Walker and my own Dad, former president of the USGA, loved this little course and loved the challenge of thirteen." President Bush's father also enjoyed another Travis course, as a member of Round Hill in Connecticut.

Designing Courses from
Georgia to Canada

By mid-January, 1921, Travis was back at the Royal Poinciana Hotel in West Palm Beach, Florida, enjoying the company of fellow Old Guard members. Travis played recreational golf with his friends, but avoided the amateur championships that he had dominated for several years. He returned north in March, free from the day-to-day involvement at *The American Golfer* and anxious to immerse himself in golf course architecture.

In April, he was back in Ontario, Canada, talking with a group of men that he had visited in 1919 regarding a new golf course for an area known as Lookout Point in Welland. The spectacular property they had secured was unlike anything Travis had worked before, consisting of two farms and a promontory that was aptly known as Observatory Point. The height of land stood 150 feet above most of the terrain that the course would occupy and from on high the mists rising from Niagara Falls 20 miles away could be seen. Although Travis had often said mountain climbing was one thing and golf clearly another, the grand possibilities that the site offered could not be ignored.

The club had originally intended to only have nine holes of golf but Travis convinced them to cultivate 18, stating that the course "has all the attributes of a World-Beater." He found the soil ideal, a rich but sandy loam cap over a bed of gravel—perfect for growing grass and draining water runoff. He situated the layout so that the club could continue to operate a vineyard and an apple orchard on the lower plain below the hillside, and club records show that for the first few years more revenue was derived from the sale of grapes than were received from green fees. Ten holes were ready for play at the grand opening on June 1, 1922, with the remainder opening shortly thereafter.

Today, Lookout Point remains a stellar example of Travis's work, lovingly maintained and enhanced in a manner that Travis would be pleased with, and proudly presented by a cordial and friendly membership that appreciates the treasure they have. The routing has

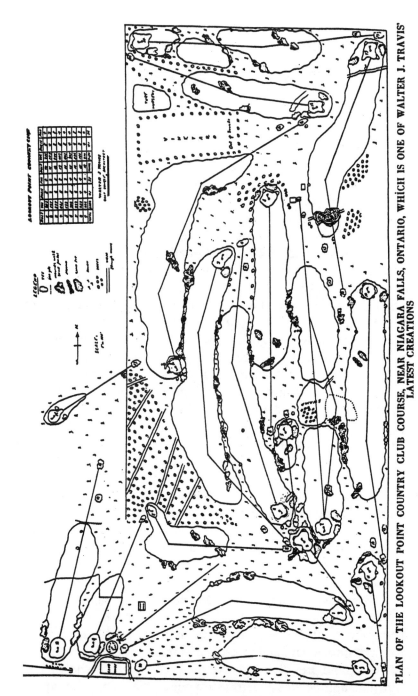

**PLAN OF THE LOOKOUT POINT COUNTRY CLUB COURSE, NEAR NIAGARA FALLS, ONTARIO, WHICH IS ONE OF WALTER J. TRAVIS'
LATEST CREATIONS**

Lookout Point features a clubhouse with a commanding view of the challenging layout below.

been changed after the original clubhouse was destroyed, and the new facility was perched on the highest point of the property. Some out-of-the way bunkers that caught wayward shots propelled away from the greens by mounding have been removed due to the enormous runoff problem that faces a course with so much elevational change.

Golf course architect Ian Andrew of Scarborough, Ontario has been working on Lookout for the last few years, and his well-conceived plan for this course and several other Travis courses in the area reveals his sensitivity to the classic elements that Travis utilized in his work. Andrew has not touched a single green at Lookout, even though some are less than 3,000 square feet. He has replaced mounds that had been removed and situated bunkers that work in conjunction with the hillocks. Lookout Point is one of the courses any Travis aficionado must visit, and host professional Gord McInnis Jr.—who together with his father has held court at Lookout for many, many years—will welcome the properly introduced visitor with classy hospitality.

With his design reputation growing in the Buffalo area, Travis was asked to look at another property in Stafford, New York—though the characteristics of the acreage was diametrically opposed to the flashy hilltop location of Lookout Point. "The general contour of the ground, undulating without being hilly, the presence of a stream and the general character of the soil all lend themselves to the creation of a first-class course in every respect," wrote Travis to the newly-organized Stafford Country Club.

Here, on a relatively level piece of land where a less-talented architect might have planned a lackluster design, Travis played one of his strong suits. As architect Ian Andrew notes, "While I talk about great greens and mounds, his ability to route a golf course might have been his strongest skill." Not one of the first nine holes that opened in 1922 runs in the same direction. The first heads southwest, the second turns north, the third runs east, and, although these are now the holes that start the back nine, so goes the layout throughout all 18 holes—turning, twisting and rolling along, first in one direction, then another; first with a long hole, then a shorty—never predictable, never rote, always engaging.

In July 1922, when nine holes were open (now the back nine), Travis wrote the club: "My first survey of the site disclosed its splen-

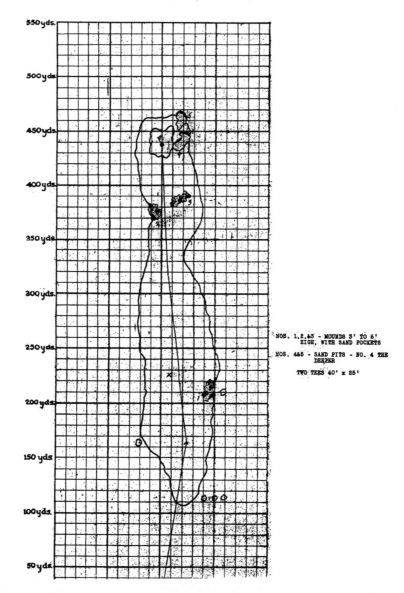

SCALE 1–100　　　EACH SQUARE – 30'

WALTER J. TRAVIS
GOLF COURSE ARCHITECT
STAFFORD COURSE – 6 HOLE 438–413 YARDS

NOS. 1,2,&3 – MOUNDS 3' TO 6'
HIGH, WITH SAND POCKETS

NOS. 4&5 – SAND PITS – NO. 4 THE
DEEPER

TWO TEES 40' x 25'

Travis provided detailed drawings with notations
for most of his clients.

This green at Stafford Country Club is typical of the elevational changes possible on the intimate putting carpets.

did, not to say magnificent possibilities. These possibilities have become actualities, in so far as the first nine holes are concerned, and have fully justified my most sanguine expectations. There are several superb holes, unsurpassed anywhere, and without a single weak one in the whole bunch." The second nine opened for play in 1929.

By now in his design evolution Travis realized that not every course could be a Garden City and capable of hosting a U.S. Open. "While it is unqualifiedly of championship caliber, I have not lost sight of the fact that for the larger part the quality of play will be quite mediocre, for some little time at least, and have accordingly 'made the punishment fit the crime' by making it as easy as possible for the duffer and, at the same time, hard for the good player, so as to make the play interesting and enjoyable for all classes."

It is one thing for a promise to be fulfilled at the time it is made, but quite another for such to hold true 80 years later. Stafford con-

LOOKING TOWARDS 15TH GREEN FROM SMALL HILL APPROXIMATELY 60YDS AWAY. TWO SETS OF CHOCOLATE DROP SAND
BUNKERS IN FOREGROUND. RAISED 16TH TEE TO RIGHT OF 15TH GREEN WITH CLUBHOUSE IN DISTANCE.

Mounding at Stafford in 1923.

tinues to be a fine members' course. Yet, in the fall of 1999, with the
tees pushed back, the greens cut down and the rough pumped up,
the Club successfully hosted the New York State Men's Senior Amateur—and six over par was the winning score.

In 1921, Travis began to reorganize his schedule in light of his
new direction and responsibilities. Devoted to architecture, he now
had multiple projects underway at the same time. Since design was
his top priority, he no longer followed the familiar patterns of his
competitive days. Instead of migrating to Florida for several winter
months, Travis used the time to optimize growing, planting, and
mapping conditions at the sites he was working with.

He resigned from the Old Guard Society, using proposed changes
to their home course as part of his excuse. In a letter to treasurer
Benjamin Rosenthal he said, "Apart from the many fine men belong-
ing to the Society, and whose companionship I shall greatly miss,
there is little in the golf there that will appeal to me. The old course

Walter Hagen putts on the 11th green at Stafford during a 1925 exhibition.

had many charms, not so much in a golfing way, but principally from the associations. With the proposed changes all this will disappear. The real wrench is the severance of relations with the Old Guard—but I will always be with you in spirit."

Although Travis no longer pined for the edge of competition, he still enjoyed the game of golf. Writing to Robert Hunter, a friend who had taken up his Eastern roots and moved to California, Travis said: "I play practically every afternoon, and am just as keen as ever—but not quite so steady."

When the USGA reversed itself in 1921 and abolished the prohibition of golf course architects from the amateur ranks, Travis, sporting a 3 handicap, was inadvertently entered into an 18-hole event at Garden City. "I played with Louis Livingston in the Handicap on Saturday," Travis wrote to Hunter, "but not as a competitor, and when we came in I found my name on the board. Rather than submit to the ignominy of 'No Card' I turned my score in...and it happened to be the best gross. I merely mention this to show the absolute distaste I have now for competitions. And yet I believe I am fonder of the game than ever."

During 1920 and 1921, Hunter tried everything he could think of to get Travis to California. First he extolled the health benefits. "I cannot tell you how sorry I am to know that you have not been well this winter. As you know, the climate in California is ideal both summer and winter, and I am quite sure it would do your general health a great deal of good to come out here for a few months."

When that didn't work, Hunter tried the financial rewards. "I think the business possibilities are great for one in your line, and if you would let it be known that you would make a visit to the Coast and would be willing to advise local committees upon greens, layout, etc., I think the visit would be a profitable one for you."

By 1921, Travis was showing some interest. "The seed thus planted is beginning to show signs of germinating. For years I have been spending the winter in Palm Beach, but am about fed up with it and now lean favorably toward California next winter, quite apart from any lure of work in my line."

But the winter of 1920–1921 came and went and Travis was still grounded on the East Coast, so Hunter tried another track—suggesting a series of highly-publicized matches with the best Pacific golfers.

"I know it would be a splendid thing from a business stand-point," Travis countered, "but business or no business, I simply loathe the mere thought of playing before a gallery. Time was when I paid no attention to that sort of thing. But now it is quite different."

Finally Hunter pulled out all the stops. "I shall certainly be more than glad to do anything I can in California to induce you to spend a winter here. I understand Del Monte is going to invite you to be its guest for as long a period as you desire to spend. It is one of the most delightful places in the world and you will enjoy every moment there. I would suggest that you put an advertisement announcing your coming. This, I think, would bring a number of demands for your services and enable you to go to work immediately upon your arrival."

Travis replied, "There is no dearth of work here in the East—I have more than I can take care of. But I should really like to build some monuments in California."

There is no record of Travis ever connecting with Hunter on the West Coast, and surely no golf courses that bear the Travis name. He did, however, enter into a correspondence with the city of Pasadena in regard to designing a municipal course—an alliance that did not produce the monument Travis was hoping for.

Juggling a Huge Work Load

By 1922, Travis was juggling at least seven projects. The projects ranged from courses at the groundbreaking stage, to others nearly ready to open. His list included North Jersey in Wayne, New Jersey; North Penn Club in Bradford, Pennsylvania; Round Hill in Greenwich, Connecticut; Yahnundasis in Utica, New York; Cherry Hill in Ridgeway, Ontario; Kirkwood Links in Camden, South Carolina; and the final completion of the two-course complex for the Biltmore Hotel in Westchester, New York.

North Jersey Country Club began as the Paterson Golf Club in April, 1894, but when the club purchased 200 acres of virgin woodland in the early 1920s, they engaged Travis to design a championship layout. This was one of Travis's most demanding sites and when 30,000 mature trees had finally been harvested, a rocky, thin-soiled expanse was discovered. The course took several years to finish, but the wait was worth it, as it complements the stately Clifford Wendehack-designed fieldstone clubhouse perfectly. Both are classy monuments that demand your attention.

Today, North Jersey remains a stern test of golf with rolling fairways surrounded by massive trees and small undulating greens at the conclusion of a diverse set of fairways. It is fitting that host pro Chris Dachisen is a former New Jersey Open champion. The ninth green at North Jersey is one of the finest examples of a multisectioned, filled-with-subtle (and not so subtle) undulations that Travis installed on many of his courses—and its open display to the clubhouse results in great entertainment for the members.

North Penn Club in the attractive mountains of northeast Pennsylvania is another interesting course that Travis was involved with during 1922. Set on a valley floor with hardwood-covered hills surrounding it in every direction, the property Travis was called to look at features a meandering creek that he used extensively in his design. Although he planned a full 18-hole course, only nine were built in 1922. The other nine were installed 36 years later by Dick Wilson. Even though Wilson followed Travis's blueprint—a document that still hangs in the clubhouse—their architectural styles could not have been farther apart, and it shows.

The Travis holes feature intimate sloping greens with curling bunkers of individual personality. The Wilson holes include broad putting surfaces with large, flat, rounded bunkers—unlike a single bunker Travis ever made. Still, the Travis routing shines through and the course is an enjoyable experience in a striking setting. The magnificent, castle-like clubhouse with its slate roof and stately turrets adds to the experience. The North Penn Club merged with the Country Club of Bradford in 1937, and today the club is known as the Pennhills Club.

Round Hill is another courtly club that Travis was involved with in 1922—set on a hillside site with dramatic elevation changes in Greenwich, Connecticut. After designing the layout, Travis turned the construction over to Alfred Tull who had built several of his other courses. In 1924, Tull placed an ad for his services in *Golf Illustrated*. When Travis saw the ad, he took issue with the way the credits were listed, thinking Tull was trying to take credit for Round Hill, North Penn, and North Jersey.

Travis fired off letters to the Round Hill's president, *Golf Illustrated*, and Tull, rejecting the claim as absolutely false. "He never had anything to do with the laying out or designing of any of them," Travis wrote. "Recently he has decided to go in for architectural work on his own account, although quite without any practical experience in this direction...and as a result my business relations with him have ceased."

When Tull received the letter, he felt he had been wronged and fired back. "I fail to see where I transgressed, there has never been on my part any intention of claiming the designing of the courses you mention. I certainly do claim full credit for their construction. If you wish I am quite willing to insert 'Designed by Walter J. Travis,' but I could hardly do so without your permission. I also note that in architectural work I am quite without practical knowledge or experience. My dear Sir, I have been studying golf course architecture for the past five years under a Master, you do scant justice to my intelligence to assume that I have handled your construction work for some years and listened to the praise, comments and criticisms of club members without gaining a lot of practical experience."

Today Round Hill remains an exclusive enclave and home to the United States Senior Golf Association annual championship each June.

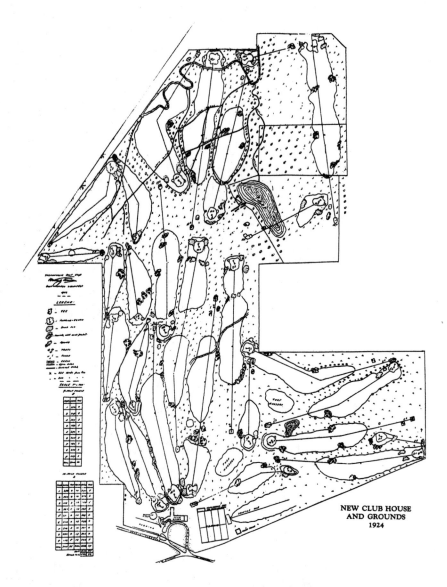

Travis planned 27 holes for Yahnundasis, today an excellent
18-hole course in Utica, New York.

With the gang at Yahnundasis—a course Travis returned to
often in the 1920s.

Travis had first visited Yahnundasis in Utica, New York in 1914
to play an exhibition match, and he returned two years later to plan
an 18-hole golf course. Travis was fond of the club and enjoyed the
company of the Sherman brothers, sons of the late vice-president
James Sherman who died suddenly in 1912. Part of the Travis course
was sold off in favor of additional land parcels with more possibility,
and The Old Man returned in 1920 to design another group of holes.
By the 1924 opening of the grand clubhouse, Travis had planned 27
holes but that number was eventually reduced to 18. Three of those
were altered in 1931, and several more needed to be modified to
accommodate the expanding New York State Thruway system in
1961. Despite all the changes, the Travis golf that remains is some
of his best.

Today's course drapes itself over a series of hills and dales, curling
and twisting through acres of trickling brooks, magnificent speci-
men trees, and bold rock outcroppings. It starts with the gorgeous
green site for the opening hole, continues past the buried elephants
on the mysterious third, then up the steep hill to the bunker-cradled

"signature" par-3 seventh, and finishes with the never-ending 560-yard ninth. All in all, the front side at Yuhnandasis is one of the most outstanding collection of holes on the planet.

But the back nine is tougher, including hikes of heart-pumping proportions. The 17th is a short par 4, but the pocket green remains completely hidden until you're practically on top of it. Many players have no strength left for the way-too-long-to-reach-in-regulation closer, and the convoluted putting green is no place to pass out. This course is a must-play for anyone wishing to understand Travis design theorem.

Travis began another Buffalo area job—Cherry Hill—late in 1922. It was to be built for a group of American golfers, but it was to be based just over the Canadian border where they all enjoyed their lakefront vacation homes. Travis inherited a rather level piece of property that the Cherry Hill club history described in the following unflattering terms: "All in all, we must agree that Mr. Travis did a remarkable job with what was then not only flat, but basically uninteresting land. The course is perfectly balanced in the sense that starting at either number one or number 10, the par for every 3 holes totals 12 strokes."

Once again Travis concocted an interesting routing for the course, despite working in the confines of a square block of land. He also utilized small greens in every shape and orientation to create diversity in the approach play. He accentuated the few variations the land would give him and framed narrow fairways with trees that would direct a more exacting play for years to come. Travis pulled out all his tricks and transformed a level field into a stimulating golfing ground.

William Harries, a golf course architect in his own right, built the layout for Travis and the quality of the work was excellent. In the modern era, Canadian architect C.E. Robinson remodeled all the bunkers on the course. Though exceedingly attractive, they are somewhat out of keeping with how Walter would have done it. Fortunately, the greens have remained original. The 3rd, 11th, and 16th are standouts.

In the Spotlight

Besides all of the other projects, Travis brought his greatest and grandest complex to life in 1922. John Bowman, president of the Pershing Square group of hotels, envisioned a community for the country's wealthiest sportsmen in Westchester, New York. In 1919, he purchased over 500 acres from the Park estate and set out to build a luxury hotel, private homes of distinction and sporting fields that would include two 18-hole golf courses. Travis's assignment was to build one course for high-caliber players and one course for the rest of the golfing public that would flock to this luxurious planned community. The thick woods, rocky outcroppings, and variegated topography gave him plenty of ammunition for the tougher test.

The Westchester Biltmore Country Club opened in May of 1922. With an initiation fee of only $25, more than 1,500 members signed up on opening day. Despite the stampede, the enterprise struggled. Just seven years later, the Club members purchased the property from developer Bowman and renamed the complex the Westchester Country Club.

The client was pleased with the product Travis produced, writing him: "All golfers who have visited our course are loud in their praise of our greens and I think that you yourself will be pleased with them. The courses when completed will be in my opinion all that you thought they would be—unique and interesting throughout. The practice putting green is a dream, admired by everyone."

Travis designed the West Course—the tougher of the two and the one currently used for the PGA Tour's Buick Classic—to be reversible. This service was one he advertised, charging $3,000 for an 18-hole layout and $4,000 for one that could be played in both directions. It was an interesting concept that allowed greenkeepers to rest their normal greens for the winter, while still allowing golfers to enjoy the challenge, and, in fact, a slightly different challenge, year-round. By selecting one enlarged teeing ground as the target, and by positioning some of the bunkers so that they accommodated and influenced play from the opposite direction, Travis built two courses from one. It was a concept so far ahead of its time, it has yet to come into vogue.

WALTER J. TRAVIS

Golf Course Architect

GARDEN CITY, L. I.

---

*Following are some of the courses
which I have designed:*

Columbia Country Club
Cherry Hill Club
Garden City Country Club
Hollywood Golf Club
Kirkwood Links
Lakewood Country Club
Lookout Point Country Club
Milwaukee Country Club
North Jersey Country Club
Onondaga G. & C. C.
Orchard Park Club
Round Hill Club
Stafford C. C.
Westchester-Biltmore C. C.
Yahnundasis G. C.

Advertisement placed in *The American Golfer* in 1921.

Both courses at Westchester have been altered through the years, initially by William Flynn. Other architects, including Alfred Tull, Perry Maxwell, Tom Winton, Joseph Finger, Stephen Kay, and Rees Jones, have all suggested, modified, remodeled, or added to what Travis left. Most recently Ken Dye has revised 13 holes on the South Course, adding 600 yards in length while rebuilding tees and bunkers. Today, the West Course receives thousands of spectators who watch the most talented pros in the world struggle to make par on

the 80-year-old holes. Four holes on the layout are listed among the most difficult holes on the PGA Tour and professional constantly remark on the power and cunning the course requires. The layout is highly praised.

Applying for a Patent on Sand

One of Travis's regular stops on his trip south was the Kirkwood Hotel in Camden, South Carolina, where golf had been played since 1903. In 1922, the hotel engaged Travis to take a part of the existing golf course and utilize it with some new acreage to create an 18-hole course. Part of the problem Travis foresaw was the greens. Although winter grass greens were being cultivated at some locations in the south, Kirkwood still relied on sand surfaces.

"On the ordinary sand green it is impossible to hold the ball on any but very short lofted approach shots; moreover, nearly all are dead level, with the hole, unchanged from season to season, in the center, making the putting deadly monotonous besides affecting the whole play," wrote Travis.

"A little over a year ago I applied myself to the problem of constructing sand greens which, to all intents and purposes, would be identical with the best turf greens, and free from the weaknesses which attach to the ordinary sand green." Travis had been experimenting with various mixtures of clay, sandy loam, and peat moss, and had built and tested five different greens. With structure to the components, Travis felt he could build undulating greens with pitch to them that would also receive an incoming shot without colossal bounces.

His figures showed that the greens that measured from four to seven thousand square feet could be built for about $400 each and that maintenance would be considerably lower than grass greens. Travis installed 18 of them on the new Kirkwood Links course, wrote about the process in the October 1923 issue of *Golf Illustrated*, tried to convince other architectural clients to try them, and then hired a lawyer to patent the idea.

The application for patent was filed on April 25, 1923, and Travis claimed to be the "first and sole inventor of the improvement in the construction of sand putting greens described and claimed in the annexed specification." Working with due deliberation, the Patent Office rejected the application in a letter of December 10 stating: "The claim is rejected as not claiming a proper process."

Thinking that he could reason with procedure, Travis wrote back to contest the decision. His comments included: "...with all respect,

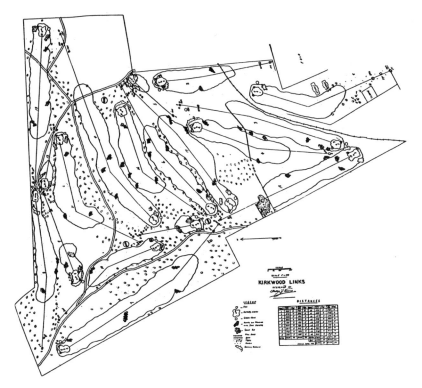

At the Kirkwood Links in Camden, South Carolina, Travis installed
improved sand greens that featured modulation
to the putting surface.

your examiner is not fully conversant with matters pertaining to
golf, as the process under notice is one of the three epochal discov-
eries in connection with the game during the last 25 years, the others being (a) the invention of the Haskell golf ball and (b) the discovery
of the vegetative method of propagating turf for greens."

The Patent Department remained unimpressed, but suggested a
competent patent attorney might be of help. The department sent
Travis a list of such in Washington, DC.

As research in southern grasses improved and overseeding became a common practice, interest in sand greens—whether undulating or not—died out. Travis never patented the idea, though there

is evidence that a few other southern clubs tried the procedure and Travis did receive some positive feedback regarding the concept. In March 1925 Travis received a letter from Carl Anderson, a landscape architect in Danbury, Connecticut. "I played the Kirkwood Links yesterday and enjoyed it so much that I felt like sending you the highest compliments for your creation. The greens hold a pitch well, are better putting than 4/5 of turf greens and present, because of their undulations, many interesting and real golf shots requiring care, touch and placement of each shot. I heartily congratulate you on your fine work and new ideas."

Kirkwood Links hired Donald Ross to modify the greens and grass them in 1938 and his sketches of the greens with notes of his plans to change them have been saved by the Club, which was renamed the Camden Country Club in 1942.

For a time the course was a fascinating blend of the two architects, featuring Travis's superior routing skills with Ross's contours to the tiny greens and bunker complexes of both. A wealth of standout holes included the second (with its unhittable green only 175 yards away), the narrow pine-tree-chute to the eighth, and the fabulous railroad-track-lined 13th. Camden was the subject of another major renovation in 1999. Results are pending.

Farther Afield

The following year found Travis engaged in projects further afield, most of which he is not known for in the same way as his 1922–1923 output. He planned an 18-hole layout for the Milwaukee Country Club in Wisconsin, but he did so via an elaborate correspondence, topographical maps, and groundwork done by men he had worked with on other projects.

His contact at Milwaukee was Louis Allis, one of the stalwart members responsible for growing the club in the early years, and he worked in conjunction with Jackson Kemper who provided design input. The construction was handled by A. Davies, who Travis had worked with before. Davies was also juggling a Louisville, Kentucky project at the same time. Travis reworked 11 existing holes and added seven new ones on the 77-acre Ilsley parcel the club had recently purchased.

Typically, he filled in the catch-all-levels-of-players cross bunkers and added options to the standard line of play on the holes he retained, adding new challenges in a modern mode. Unfortunately, the new course involved heroic carries, walks up steep embankments, and a ninth green that was 300 yards from the clubhouse. The membership rebelled. Just four years later, the club employed Charles Alison of the firm of Colt and Alison to install another course—a layout that used virtually none of the holes Travis had planned, and a layout that became the basis for the course that is played today. This was the shortest-lived Travis course ever installed.

At the Country Club of New Canaan in southern Connecticut, Travis left some design changes in the hands of William Tull, brother of Alfred, and a soil and turf expert who built many of the layouts his brother would design. But a miserable winter and spring, together with what Travis perceived as fumbling and perhaps deception, combined to delay the work and pad the bill. Travis wrote Marshal Stearns, head of the construction committee, "It is rather a singular fact, that on the last job or so, when Tull has gone in for a little nepotism and dragged one or more members of his family into the undertakings or what not, the cost estimates have been exceeded. I am never going to employ Tull again."

Travis suggested that Emilio 'Mollie' Strazza, the superintendent at Round Hill, finish the job, but the six greens that he suggested alteration to were the only ones on the Willie Park Jr. course
that were altered. And since then, changes by Tull, Robert Trent
Jones, and others have blurred any Travis identity in the layout.

In 1924, Travis was also contacted for a consultation regarding
the Yountakah Country Club in Nutley, New Jersey, by club president F.S. Dickinson. Travis composed a long, thoughtful response to
several questions that the club was wrestling with to locate a new
clubhouse and thus rearrange the holes to start and end at the new
location.

The course, which had existed since Tom Bendelow plotted it in
1897, was slowly being pressed by the expansion of roads, housing,
and business interests. Travis suggested, "If this continues, as seems
likely, the time will not be far distant when your property will so
increase in value that the taxes will become burdensome...to say
nothing of the possibility of public roads being projected through
the course. This possibility has got to be faced. The same thing has
happened elsewhere. Having regard to what seems to be inevitable,
I would venture to offer the suggestion that "new pastures" be found,
that options be secured on one or two sites for a new and more
modern course, infinitely better than the present one could possibly
be developed into." Yountakah did not take Travis's recommendations to heart, and in 1943 the parcel was sold to ITT and the Club
ceased to exist.

Oak Ridge Argument

During this time, Travis found himself in the middle of a conflict with the Oak Ridge Golf Club in Tuckahoe, New York, a dispute that eventually resulted in lawsuits being filed on behalf of both parties. Travis had reconstructed their golf course. During the process, greenkeeper Melville had asked about joining Travis to pursue golf course construction work. Travis claimed he advised Melville to divide his time between greenkeeping at Oak Ridge and new work Travis could provide, but Melville resigned his position instead. Oak Ridge claimed Travis had enticed Melville to leave. Tull had performed some faulty work and there were problems with the new greens, tees, and fairways. When the Club withheld the final $500 payment from Travis's fee of $2,500, Travis claimed there was no basis for the shortage and that no problems had been brought forth before Melville's departure.

Travis employed New York City attorney John Ward to sue the Club for the balance, refuting all their claims. The Club was alleging that several greens were not draining properly due to undersurface hollows that permitted an accumulation of water; that bunkers hadn't been engineered correctly; that seed used in the fairways was old and germination was poor; and that the Club had to spend $250 to level several tees that had settled. Oak Ridge attorney Henry Fluegelman concluded that in refusing to address their concerns, Travis had willfully broken his contract and Oak Ridge planned not only to withhold the final payment but also to countersue for breach.

Travis concluded a February, 1925 letter to Ward by saying, "Speaking of Melville, it is rather a singular thing that until the episode with him occurred, everything went swimmingly in my relations with Oak Ridge, but after that—the deluge." What Travis didn't know was that Ward had unexpectedly passed away in January. When his partner Robert Oliver took over his work, there was a backlog of cases pending and Oliver estimated it would be 1926 before the matter would reach the courts. The suit was duly filed with the appropriate courts, in Travis's mind mainly to clear his name, but the outcome is unclear.

Besides bluegrass, Kentucky was known for the best hickory shafts made in the United States during the early years of golf in this country, and the Louisville Country Club is one of the oldest clubs in the south—a course was in use as early as 1896. Travis was contacted in 1924 and asked to renovate nine of the 18 existing holes, and plan an additional 18-hole course for the Club. In directing Davies to install several new bunker complexes of a modern type, Travis wrote: "You of course understand that I am not asking you to reproduce or absolutely copy any of the originals, but merely to take them as a pattern and embody the general ideas, endeavoring to have each one a little different. The dimensions and angles as specified in the plan you will follow, also the heights, but the rest is left entirely to your own artistic taste."

The renovation work was completed by September of 1924, but the additional 18-hole course never came to pass. Over the years, Louisville CC was modified by William Langford, Theodore Moreau, William Diddel, and Benjamin Wihry. Little of Travis's work remains to be enjoyed.

A Lesson for Bobby

One of Travis's regular southern haunts was the Augusta Country Club in Georgia—the turn-of-the-century club that abuts what would eventually become Augusta National's Amen Corner. The Club utilized two courses at the time and Travis planned the renovation of one green on the Lake Course in 1924, believing it would lead to the modification of four others that needed help and perhaps eventually to a complete renovation of the facility.

Club president Fielding Wallace wrote Travis to thank him for his work in April, 1924. "It was certainly very good of you to give so much of your time and to go to so much trouble when you were off on a trip of recreation and pleasure. We will always be deeply grateful for it and for your interest in the general welfare of our club."

In his contacts with Augusta, Travis was asked to speak to young Bobby Jones, already a force to be reckoned with on the national stage but still lacking some of the skills that would take him to the pinnacle of American golf. Travis had watched Jones play in his first national championship at Merion and remarked that the lad "would never improve upon his shotmaking but might better learn the occasions upon which they should be played...and his putting method was faulty." Colonel Jones, the lad's father, arranged a meeting between the two champions. When Jones was 15 minutes late to his first audience with Travis, however, The Old Man huffed away and indicated that if Jones was to receive his advice, he'd better show up on time for his lesson. At the time, Jones was having trouble with his putting and Travis was still regarded as something of an expert.

A second meeting was arranged and this time Jones was waiting. In his book, *The Life and Times of Bobby Jones*, Syd Matthews offered this version of the encounter. "It was in the locker room of the Augusta Country Club in 1924 that Jones finally received, in the guise of a lecture, the putting lesson which changed the course of Jones's golfing history. Travis explained to Bob that he must get his feet so close together that the heels almost touch. Then he must take the club back with his left hand in a longer sweeping stroke with what appears to be hinged wrists working in opposition to each other. He changed his putting grip, overlapping the index finger of the left hand, not the right. With his new putting stroke, Jones became the Mechanical Man of Golf."

When speaking about putting, Jones would sometimes say, "I went seven years before I ever broke into the big time—and it was mainly missing little putts that ruined me. So I started trying to learn to putt, and a certain old gentleman whom you may have heard of—Mr. Walter J. Travis—gave me two fundamental tips down in the locker room of the old clubhouse at Augusta, Georgia, and they changed me from a terrible putter into a fairly good one."

Pictures of Jones from that point on clearly show he never forgot to keep his heels together and the results speak for themselves. Although Jones had captured his first U.S. Open prior to the lesson, after it Jones went on a tear, winning every championship in sight, culminating in the Grand Slam of 1930. After that amazing accomplishment, Mrs. Travis sent her congratulations and Jones responded warmly, remembering the lesson that changed his career.

A Growing Reputation

The last few years of Walter J.'s life was filled with more golf course design work, much of it brought on by public exposure to the courses he had planned since devoting himself full-time to the pursuit.

The smallest project he ever handled, on the most unusual piece of property he ever manipulated, was a nine-hole course for the Granliden Hotel in Sunapee, New Hampshire. The correspondence regarding the course, however, was the longest of any project with which he was involved, as Travis and Dr. J.R. Nilsen swapped multiple letters about the design, installation, grow-in, and future maintenance of the pint-sized course.

Casual play began at the Granliden in 1898, and less than a decade later golf professional Alex Findlay devised a more substantial layout. But the owners were still not satisfied. The October 2, 1925 issue of the *New Hampshire Argus and Spectator* noted, "This fall guests are very much interested in the golf course at the back of the Granliden hotel where many thousands of dollars are being spent to make this one of the best in New Hampshire. The course was laid out by Walter J. Travis, the well known golf expert. The final seeding with creeping bent is now being done and it is expected the course will be in fine shape by the time the hotel opens in the spring."

The site is one of the oddest pieces of property to support nine holes one could imagine. Visualize a two-hole-wide strip of green grass that, over the course of one-half-mile, climbs 150 feet straight up. The description from 1925 rings just as true today: "From the level ground near the hotel the course rises gradually till at the 6th tee a considerable elevation is reached from which the view of Lake Sunapee is very fine, and distant mountains are to be seen in both Vermont and New Hampshire, with the intervening hills and lesser mountains making a wonderful picture. From this point the course descends till at the 9th hole the player finds himself back at the hotel."

There is substantial basis for the myth that Granliden golf disappeared forever. In the 1930s the hotel faltered, the victim of the hard times that plagued the country. During World War II, the course was neglected for lack of funds and the entire property was eventually sold to a Jesuit order. Although the Jesuits closed the grounds to the public, they continued to maintain the golf course. But since the layout is tucked away from main roads and far from the beaten paths, few knew it was there.

In the 1970s, the decrepit hotel was torn down and the property was sold at public auction. The course was one of the attractions that interested the developers who purchased the acreage, and they set out to establish a condominium community. Slowly, the golf course was restored and members began to appreciate the tiny gemstone they enjoy today.

The course is a pleasure to play, thanks in large part to the maintenance efforts of manager David Little. At 2,280 yards (par-32), Granliden is the shortest course Travis planned but all the elements of his larger courses are in evidence.

At the same time that he was crafting the intimate Granliden, Travis was developing one of his grandest projects, the Country Club of Scranton in Pennsylvania. For his normal fee of $125 plus expenses, Travis arrived in Scranton at the behest of C.F. Woolworth during the first few days of June 1925 to inspect several sites the Club was interested in developing.

Travis chose the Dr. Thompson tract of land, preferring its views, optimum site for a clubhouse, lakeside location and gentle rolling nature. He dismissed the other properties as uninviting and substandard.

Travis warned of the stony nature of the soil, but surmised that was the character of all the soil around Scranton and that once the turf was established this problem would be moot. Travis planned a wonderful golf course for the Club, and one that has been lovingly maintained and improved in the Travis spirit ever since. Once again the routing was masterful. It removed golfers from the high point of the property—the clubhouse—out into the body of the course and then spun the players this way and that as the layout marched to the farthest spot from the clubhouse, the sixth tee. Weaving their way back, enthusiasts were cast away again with holes that utilized the gentle slope of the land to maximum advantage. Established in 1896, the Club played various casual layouts until Travis performed his work. Afterward, they attracted the best golfers in the country to the first Anthracite Open in 1939. With a purse of $5,000, the tour-

The seaside property at Jekyll Island gave Travis an opportunity
to plot a natural linksland course.

nament received more entries than the U.S. Open. Henry Picard prevailed in the first event, and Sam Snead won the second against a field that included Ben Hogan, Ralph Guldahl, Lloyd Mangrun, Denny Shute, Porky Oliver, and Byron Nelson. All praised the Travis design. More recent praise has come from member and Masters tournament winner Art Wall Jr. and architect Dr. Michael Hurdzan, who added nine holes to the facility in 1991.

Travis had initially visited the coastal islands of Georgia in 1900, two years after Willie Dunn had laid out the first golf holes at the newly formed Jekyll Island Club. Travis had offered improvement suggestions at the time. When he returned in 1926, he formalized his directions and the Club instituted the changes. This led to the Oceanside Nine, still part of today's 36-hole complex.

The nearby Sea Island Golf Club was so impressed with the natural links that Travis had produced at Jekyll Island that they invited him to St. Simons Island to install nine holes there in 1927. The Plantation Nine was a commanding walk through massive oak and magnolia trees, with Spanish moss hanging from the sentinels and tidal inlets snaking into the fairways to provide visual delight and shotmaking challenges. Travis built bigger bunkers than his usual style to reflect the scale of the property, and Sea Island used his course as the centerpiece for their expanding resort.

Although elegantly maintained, the Travis nine was manipulated by a host of architects through the years, including Colt and Alison who visited two years later and cast many of the holes in their image while they tacked on another nine holes. Since the early years, the layout has been modified by Robert Trent Jones and—more recently—by Rees Jones, who modernized the holes with the flair and feel that characterizes his remodeling work.

The last two projects that Travis was part of brought him back to the Northeast and close to his beloved Manchester and the Ekwanok Country Club where he had spent at least two weeks of each summer since 1899.

The impetus for the establishment of Ekwanok was that the old Equinox Links was not of high enough quality to support the esteemed clientele that frequented Manchester in the summer months. The first golfing ground had been a "crude six-hole course with fairways carved through prairie weed, tamaracks, and a swamp in a rough field behind the hotel," according to designer George Orvis's own admission. But Orvis secured a second piece of property between the hotel and the Battenkill River and installed six new holes, which eventually grew to 18. As Ekwanok began to attract all the better players, the Equinox course fell into disrepair and was not much more than a practice field until July of 1925. That was when the rejuvenated Equinox Company proudly announced that they had "begun the construction of an eighteen hole golf links on its lands east of Main Street in the village. Walter J. Travis, the well known golfer has laid out the links and work on them will be pushed as rapidly as possible this summer." Work did not progress much in 1925, and weather conditions conspired against the project over the winter and early spring of 1926 as well.

Failing Health

By the summer of 1926, Travis's health was failing him, as his bronchial condition had worsened, and his doctor had advised him to cut back on his active design business. It is possible he had other afflictions as well. In an article that appeared in the *Buffalo Evening News* on May 25, 1947, Grantland Rice, describing Travis's condition wrote, "Well over 60, he had a temperature of 102 the last round I played with him. He confided that day that he had tuberculosis and his doctors gave him less than six months to live, unless he gave up golf and went to Saranac or Arizona. 'I'd rather have six months of golf, than 50 years without it,' he said." Travis was happy to spend a low-key summer supervising construction of the Equinox course and playing golf when he could at Ekwanok.

Travis felt better as the summer moved along, good enough to consider planning another golf course in nearby Troy. He returned to Garden City for the winter, despite suggestions that Arizona or Colorado would be better for his condition.

The grand opening of the Equinox course was postponed until 1927. Although he wasn't well enough to play, Travis followed the action, mostly from the front seat of a car that was driven to the holes that were accessible.

An exhibition match between Jess Sweetser and Francis Ouimet was played on Sunday, July 3, 1927, and it marked the second birth of the Equinox Links. Travis had not seen Sweetser since he had become the second American to win the British Amateur, 22 years after Travis had worked the trick. At the Equinox, Sweetser came within two strokes of equaling the par of 73 and beat Ouimet by nine, in part because Francis "was frequently off the course." The *Manchester Journal* also noted the attendance of Travis. "The Grand Old Man of golf was in Manchester for the formal opening of the club and watched the exhibition match. When it is considered that it is less than two years ago that Mr. Travis began to plan the course and but 10 months since the first grass seed was sown, the course is a wonderful exhibit of what can be accomplished under proper supervision."

Equinox remained in original Travis condition until 1992, when the Guinness Corporation purchased the hotel with the golf course

Mr. Walter J. Travis driving from the eleventh tee at Equinox

Travis loved Ekwanok, and returned every summer for
rounds with his usual companions.

and wished to see the course updated to modern world-class standards, as a sister property to their holdings at Gleneagles in Scotland.

Rees Jones was brought in to look at the property in the spring of 1991. "It's so nice when you have a gorgeous setting like that with the mountain backdrop. The land lays there perfectly for golf and Travis did a good job with the routing. But the course was opened right before the Depression and they might have run out of money to finish it.

"One of the reasons people call me is that I try to utilize design features that I think are redeeming. That's the way Travis had the bunkers, that was his style. But the brook was unfairly placed so as to penalize the average golfer. Back then they didn't pipe them for economic reasons." Jones removed a creek that influenced more than half the holes. Unable to add length due to confining land restraints, he compensated with increased bunkering. The result is a fine reworking of a great old course.

The final letter that Travis wrote to a client was on June 22, 1927, when he corresponded with J.S. Melville of the Country Club of Troy. "When I got knocked under, early in May," Travis wrote, "the doctors told me I must get out to Colorado and Arizona quickly, that staying in the East, under the most expert treatment, would in effect, at the best, a slight improvement. Poor simple fool, I thought I knew better.

"Dispassionately comparing my present condition with that of June 3, I make the astounding discovery that I'm only the merest trifle improved, and that it is folly to stay around here, influenced by the fact that although Mr. Stone and Mr. Gallagher write exceedingly nice letters, I know they must be greatly worried as to whether things will be all right for the planting and seeding when the proper time comes around for the work.

"So come down in your car as soon as it suits you (any day will suit me), stay the night and we will be on our way the next morning. Engage a quiet room at the hotel, with as little stair climbing as possible—quiet more particularly for the other fellow, as I cough pretty near all night—and, if possible, with a fairly comfortable armchair in which one can perhaps arrange to sleep. Lying down chokens me. Then you will have to arrange with one of your men to drive from hole to hole with me. I'm pretty weak."

Travis planned a return to Manchester for the opening match at the Equinox, "from where my son-in-law, George N. Emory, will bring me back home, and a few days later will find me bound Westward Ho!"

Final Days in Denver

Jack and Nan (as they called each other) arrived in Denver on July 19, 1927, and quietly took an apartment at the Hotel Ayres at 1441 Logan Street. No one who might have been interested in the fact that Travis was in the city knew he was there, and his health now precluded him from going out at all.

On July 26, Anne wrote to their daughter Adelaide and described her Dad's condition. "I read him the morning papers and he sits there for an hour, then back to bed. Sleep like the dead till noon. Then gets on the upside down bed and coughs up the flem. Then back to bed and sleep. After lunch he naps, then I read to him for hours and then more sleep. He sat up a while this afternoon and then the nurse gets him ready for bed at eight."

Travis still had his sense of humor however. When Anne made out a check to pay the nurse, he wanted to be sure that she told their daughter about it. "He wanted me to write you that 'It was the first cheque I ever made out.'"

He enjoyed a telegram he received from his nephew, Bert. "Lots of love for Uncle Walter," he wrote. "Tell him he has been in lots of tougher matches than this and won out."

But the Schenectady couldn't save his skin this time, and Walter J. Travis died quietly in his sleep in the early morning hours of Sunday, July 31, 1927. Anne was at his side. His daughter Adelaide, who had become alarmed at her mother's last letter, when she wrote, "Tell Ad she'd better come out. Dad not so well. Don't know how things will turn," had left New York for Denver, but arrived several hours after he passed away. According to his wishes, Walter J. was cremated in Denver at the Riverside Cemetery. The family then began the journey back to the Dellwood Cemetery in Manchester where Travis wished to be buried.

Condolences and accolades for Travis were delivered to Anne, and tributes filled the print media. Chick Evans wrote, "I always think of him as a quiet, reserved person whom everyone respected and to whom no one ever got very close. No man in his time exercised a more potent influence on the game, or stood higher as a player. To the youngsters of that period he was a figure to worship.

In the last few months of his life, Travis was resigned to
watching the action rather than creating it.

Whether he will be known as a great golf architect time alone can tell, but his reputation as a great golfer rests secure."

Travis's son Bartlett echoed Evan's view. "He was the Spartan type with an English background, taught never to show his emotions. His reserve never let down. It awed me and I had been taught not to push myself where I wasn't invited."

A. Linde Fowler added, "He played the game of life and death exactly as he played his game of golf, showing nothing of what his innermost feelings might be. Only a few weeks ago I saw Mr. Travis for the last time. Even then I was told that Mr. Travis probably would not live a year, yet no one ever could have suspected, from his cheerful mien and keen-eyed attention to the play, that he was the least bit disturbed over a physical condition which he undoubtedly knew made his days numbered."

Jerome Travers noted, "He was always pleasant to play with. He didn't say much in the course of a round, but he always played squarely, he never took advantage of his opponent and he never tried to disconcert or upset an opponent. There is no question but what he was the greatest putter that ever lived."

He played many matches at Nassau with William Hicks who said: "Mr. Travis was a delightful man to play with. We had many an interesting golf match. The golf world has lost one of its greatest figures."

At 11:30 A.M. on Sunday, August 7, Reverend David Cunningham-Graham performed a simple ceremony in the lobby of the clubhouse at the new Equinox Links. Travis was not a religious man, but he had a pleasant personal relationship with the pastor of the Manchester Congregational Church, and his brief blessings were most appropriate. A procession brought the remains to a plot just inside the gates at the Dellwood Cemetery, not far from his first golf course design and a favorite playground of his for more than 25 years. Golfers at Ekwanok paused in their play for five minutes during the service, and the Equinox Links was completely closed for the day. His family was there, as were golfing friends from Garden City, Ekwanok, and throughout New England.

Life After Walter

When the funeral was over Anne Bent Travis returned to Garden City. Son Bartlett, now 33 years old, had married Elise Stanton Hayes in January, 1926, and they were living above Kripps Pharmacy on Franklin Avenue in Garden City. Daughter Adelaide had married George North Emory in 1922. Their third child, Josephine was born in 1927, joining George North Jr. who was five, and Adelaide, age four.

Besides his golfing legacy, Travis also left a substantial bank account to keep his widow comfortable. She lived in the house they had shared for 27 years at 93 9th Street for another two years after his death, then moved into the Garden City Hotel. She traveled south in the winters—often to the Charleston, Virginia area—and stayed at the Kirby House in Sharon, Connecticut for part of the summer. She died in her daughter's home in Sharon on November 15, 1946, after a month-long illness, at the age of 83.

Daughter Adelaide and her husband occupied the Garden City house from 1929 until 1932, when they moved to Sharon, Connecticut, but retained ownership of the property. Bartlett and Elise moved to Red Springs Harbour in Glen Cove on Long Island where they had a son they named Irving Bartlett. They returned to occupy the old family home in 1936, shortly before their daughter Elise Ann (Winkie) was born. Bartlett and his family lived in the Travis home until 1957. Both Bartlett and Adelaide died in 1960. Today, Winkie Roessler is one of the last links to the Travis legacy. Her cousin Adelaide, who had most of the remaining Travis papers, passed away in 1998. Before she died she donated 100 love letters between Jack and Nan, written while they were courting in 1889, and correspondence regarding his architectural business in the 1920s, to the USGA.

Although she was only 10 when her grandmother died, Winkie remembers her as a tall, stately, and very loving woman who always had a smile on her face and a pleasant disposition. "My mother had to warn me, 'Don't ask for things from Granny (which is how all the grandchildren referred to her) because she'll get them for you.' As a 10-year-old I figured why not ask?" recalls Winkie.

238

Anne Bent, his wife of nearly 30 years, was a
cheerful and enjoyable soul.

Much of the material from the house in Garden City was donated to the Garden City Golf Club where the Travis Room pays
tribute to the Club's famous member. Unfortunately, the Schenectady
putter that was bought during the 1918 Red Cross auction was sto-
len in 1952. Thieves broke into the glass display case that housed
the famous club and made off with one of the great pieces of golf
history. It has yet to be recovered.

In 1979, Winkie and her cousin Adelaide were on hand when Walter J. Travis was inducted into the Golf Hall of Fame in Pinehurst, North Carolina. Today, he is honored in the Golf Hall of Fame at the World Golf Village in St. Augustine, Florida.

The Walter Travis Society

The Travis story may have ended there if it weren't for the efforts of Ed Homsey of Rochester, New York. A member of the Stafford Country Club, Homsey had developed an interest in the golfing accomplishments of Travis. He was particularly fascinated with the distinctive characteristics that he associated with Travis-designed golf courses. Homsey's vision was to form an alliance of Travis-designed clubs that would serve to promote a greater awareness and appreciation of the history and traditions shared by the member clubs. He felt that such a partnership would honor this remarkable man who had contributed so greatly to the development of golf in this part of the world. The centerpiece of Homsey's proposal was an inter-club golf competition. During the time when the proposal was in its formative stage, the Rochester area was in frenzy in preparation for the 1995 Ryder Cup Matches at Oak Hill Country Club. Thus, the notion of establishing a Travis Cup competition patterned after the Ryder Cup seemed a natural.

Homsey mailed his proposal to six clubs in Central and Western New York, and Southern Ontario. Initial responses lauded the idea but reserved commitment. The breakthrough for acceptance of the proposal came in a letter expressing great interest from Brian McDonald of Lookout Point Country Club in southern Ontario. McDonald, together with Dr. Joe DiVincentis, Golf Chairman of Orchard Park Country Club, extended an invitation for an organizational meeting to be held at Orchard Park.

On October 8, 1994, the initial organizational meeting was held with a group of representatives from each club. Representing Lookout Point Country Club were Archie Hood and Gord McInnis, Golf Professional. Orchard Park Country Club was represented by Dr. Joe DiVincentis, Pat Kerrigan, Mark Kirk, Golf Professional, and Tim Minahan, General Manager. Representing Stafford Country Club were Ed Homsey and Chris Sayre. The meeting was memorable for the great spirit of cooperation and enthusiasm. By acclamation, the group agreed that establishing the Travis Cup competition would create a splendid opportunity to recognize and honor the spectacular golfing feats and accomplishments of Walter J. Travis, as well as to promote and celebrate the common heritage of the clubs. The first Travis Cup was scheduled for Orchard Park Country Club in August of 1995.

George Nichols introduced the idea of establishing an historical society that would explore, collect, protect, and distribute documents establishing the accomplishments and contributions by Travis. This suggestion raised the question of whether any Travis descendants existed, and, if so, whether they would support the formation of a historical society.

The inaugural Travis Cup event at Orchard Park CC was, for the most part, a huge success. The OPCC staff and members performed the role of host superbly. Unfortunately, they were unable to control the weather. On two occasions, the competition was dramatically interrupted by severe thunderstorms that raked the course with torrential rains, lightning, and thunder. Under the most trying and difficult conditions, the competitors retreated from, and valiantly returned to the competition only to find that the playing conditions had become impossible. The event was foreshortened to a nine-hole competition. Nonetheless, the spirit of the event was not dampened as the competitors and spectators gathered to celebrate the day, and award the winners. Lookout Point Country Club was the first to have its name inscribed on the elegant new Travis Cup trophy.

The discovery that the Pennhills Club in Bradford, Pennsylvania was a Travis course led to their participation in the Travis Cup in 1996. Further discussions to formalize the Walter Travis Society took place. After several more meetings, a nonprofit organization was established in 1996. After a logo was chosen and a bank account was opened, the Travis Society became a reality.

The next several years were spent defining the goals of the organization, collecting information about Travis, identifying Travis courses and hunting for relatives—a trail that had grown cold in the 70 years since Walter J.'s death.

Eventually, Winkie Roessler was located in Vermont and the process to compile a book that would honor her grandfather's accomplishments was undertaken. In the last few years, the organization has grown by reaching out to individual members and through contacts with other clubs designed by Travis throughout the country. A collection of Travis material has been assembled, the Travis Cup has grown, and slowly the stature of The Old Man is being raised to its appropriate place in the history of American golf. The publication of this book marks the centennial of the first of three U.S. Amateur titles that Travis won, and it's an appreciation for all that he did for all lovers of the royal and ancient game.

Design Philosophy

In the span of 28 years, Travis was involved architecturally with 48 golf courses. At approximately 13 of those, he consulted on design by casually or formally suggesting changes to greens, tees, fairways, or bunkers. Some were instituted, some were not.

Travis took the changes he suggested and actually implemented them through a remodeling program at another six layouts. The most extensive work among these was his manipulations at Garden City. On at least three occasions, Travis made changes in the playing of his home club. Many of those changes are either still in place today, or have recently been restored by architect Tom Doak, who has consulted for Garden City for nearly 10 years.

Travis designed three nine-hole courses, and two of those—Granliden in New Hampshire and West Potomac Park in Maryland—closely resemble his intentions. He also planned 25 other full-size facilities, including 27 holes at Yahnundasis and 36 holes at Westchester. Some of those have gone out of existence, and others have been remodeled to death and are hardly distinguishable as a Travis golf course. However, 20 championship-length 18-hole golf courses remain today, and from them we can draw a pretty clear picture of his design style. We also have a rich literature of his ideas, as he probably wrote as much about golf course design as all but a few modern architects. Written theories are interesting. However, as Travis might have said it, "Paper is one thing, but working in the dirt is clearly another."

One defining feature that always shines on any Travis course that *hasn't* been modernized is his greens. "He really divided the greens up into small target areas by using ridge lines and valleys," says Dr. Mike Hurdzan. "And the greens are not very big either, but a lot of them were built into hills so that the ball would bounce off the hill and work back toward the greens. His greens would be considered a little severe by today's standards but considering when he did them, I think the greens really showed a lot of understanding of the strategy of the game."

"Every golf architect's designs emphasize the parts of the game which he feels are most important—which are usually those at which he is the most skilled," writes Tom Doak. "So it should be no surprise that Travis' designs are noted for superbly contoured greens and for their demand on the short game, as well as putting. The greens at Country Club of Troy, Cape Arundel and Hollywood are as intricate as any I've played on, and they have stayed very well preserved over the years."

Geoffrey Cornish points out that the beauty of the greens was more than skin deep. "For the early years, he was keenly aware of the need for both interior and surface drainage of greens. I have tried to retain the contours of his putting surfaces as he had them. Studying his book, I was impressed and amazed by his recommendations for preparing seed beds. Knowledge on that subject was hard to come by at the beginning of this century. Yet, his specifications would produce an excellent seed bed today."

"He built wonderful undulating greens with fascinating pin positions," writes Ian Andrew. "In my view, the only problem is with the size—many at Lookout Point are not even 3,000 square feet."

One of the joys of his convoluted, intimate, and multisectioned greens is the way those folds, pockets, and ridge lines are reflected out into the surrounds. This is done by the use of mounding that goes with the direction of the flow that is established on the green, and then reflected and amplified by the contours immediately adjacent.

Every course has at least one green that makes even the most jaded player step back and survey the entire package. Many are in awe as they point out little hollows, proceed to roll balls along little separations to see which way they run, and marvel at impossible pin positions that must be reserved for club championship days.

And then there's a Travis trademark—the swale green. With its roots in North Berwick in Scotland, Travis found a place on nearly every course for a green with a deep swale cutting through the surface on a diagonal. It separated the carpet into two halves and influenced nearly every putt ever made there—not to mention how it forced players to think about their approach when they were standing in the fairway. Since this was often the most controversial green on the course, many have been removed or softened so much that they are barely recognizable. Fortunately, some have been preserved intact.

The orientation of a Travis green was never the same; the shape and the size did not follow a pattern, either. But frequently there was that hollow swath, usually aligned from right rear to left front. Not sure what they look like? You can find one at the 383-yard, par-4 third at Cherry Hill, the 534-yard, par-5 17th at North Jersey, the 460-yard, par-5 16th at Hollywood, the 398-yard, par-4 sixth at Lookout Point, the 360-yard, par-4 at Granliden (the most exaggerated of all the examples), and finally—the mother of them all—the double swale on the 399-yard, par-4 seventh at Scranton.

But just as Travis felt many people maligned the rest of his game by concentrating on what a great putter he was, his courses had much more going for them than just great greens. "His strongest feature?" asked Ian Andrew of Ontario who is carefully upgrading three of his courses. "Lookout Point has simply the greatest mounds I've seen at any club to date. The mounds at the three clubs are very unique and are impressive in both scale and character. Other architects, such as Stanley Thompson, have produced mounds nearly as imaginative and impressive, but Walter Travis's mounds are still more grand than all others. The mounds are like small mountain ranges. They are not even and round, but instead feature scallops, secondary peaks and long ridgelines. The mounds also rise very quickly and steeply from existing grade just like a mountain range. While not maintenance friendly (the primary reason for their disappearance), they have greater visual impact."

When Travis designed Ekwanok in 1899, nearly every bunker in the United States looked the same. Most crossed the linear progress of the hole, forcing golfers to lift a straight shot directly over them to continue toward the putting surface. There were few pot bunkers, few hazards that were lateral, and virtually none that caused the golfer to pause and think of his strategy.

"I think he set up his bunkering very, very well," notes Hurdzan. "If you drove the ball right at certain bunkers then certain hole locations would open up and you had to play his golf courses from the hole locations backwards. You had to see where the flag was on the green and then devise a strategy from there."

As much as he wanted to impress people with his designs, Travis was also a practical man. He considered the economy of proper construction and worked within the limitations that the site suggested. "The depth of bunkers at Garden City seems to be random. Some fairway bunkers are deep, others are not. But in trying to recreate them, we did find a method to them," reveals Doak. "The workmen simply dug down until they hit the coarse gravel subsoil! That way, they didn't spread the gravel around and have to clean it up later. If there was two feet of topsoil, Travis built a two-foot-deep bunker. Four feet equaled a more difficult recovery."

And then there was the routing. "While I talk about his great greens and mounds, his ability to route a golf course might have been his strongest skill. His routings all make fantastic use of the undulations to get the best holes out of the land," says Andrew.

Travis never took a lazy approach to the routing of the course. If a big broad plain needed to be part of the plan, he never built a series of back-and-forth holes and then moved the course to another section of the property. Instead he would use part of that meadow to get somewhere else, then visit it again on the way home, so that even if holes were adjacent and similar, the golfer would play one early and return to the area later and play the other.

Seldom did golfers stand on the tee and wonder, 'Haven't we already played this hole?' For even if the site forced a similarity to some of the holes, like Donald Ross, Travis would vary the exact requirements of each test. One hole might bend ever so slightly left, another right. One drive zone would be tilted so the ball was below your feet, the next so it was slightly above. One hole might play into the prevailing wind, the other against it. Travis used all these tools to create diversity and the result is that not one course he designed is boring or tedious. All are fun, challenging, and interesting.

Although one might argue that Travis was blessed with tremendous sites, in many cases when he was approached by a club to make property inspections, he had two sites to choose from and was clearly an excellent judge of what land would work the best. In several of his correspondences with clubs, he simply informed them that the one site they had available would not yield a golf course of the caliber that he built.

Although Travis was highly regarded by the other architects of the day, his star has faded in the years since. Had he lived longer and produced a greater body of work, his place in the order of merit would be higher. Andrew had a good analogy. "In my view, he is similar to George Thomas. George Thomas was a great architect, but if you're not from California you will not likely be familiar with his great legacy of golf courses. Thomas was every bit as good as

Tillinghast or Ross, but had much less exposure due to regional isolation. The same goes for Travis."

Nevertheless, architects who have made a study of the history of their profession know his place. "I think Travis was a very important person," say Hurdzan. "He was articulate and he shared his views through his writing, so I think that definitely had an influence on people around him."

"Travis was responsible for the final product at Ekwanok and also the complete remodeling of Garden City," notes Cornish. "I rank both layouts as 'Landmarks,' the group of courses that profoundly influenced golf course architecture in North America and elevated it from functional to masterpiece."

Travis Tidbits

Despite being known for his accuracy, including rounds
that Grantland Rice documented when he hit
directional flags or flagsticks as many as five times,
Travis never recorded a hole-in-one.

In the 1920s, Travis devised a 25-question interview sheet
for applicants of the position of greenkeeper, including:
Do you favor rolling greens? Which is the better time
for seeding—spring or fall? What is the best method for
preventing crabgrass getting into your greens?
How often should greens be fertilized?

Travis drank Old Crow Rye Whiskey which he ordered by
the 10-gallon keg from the Mallard Distilling Company
in New York and bottled himself.

When R.A. Oakley of the USGA Green Committee asked to change
some wording in an article Travis had written for their Bulletin
on the fifth hole at Columbia, he responded, "Let the
5th Hole article go "as is"—or kill it, whichever you
prefer. It really makes no difference to me."

On January 17, 1903, while playing with Bruce Price and
Arden Robbins at the Garden City Golf Club, Travis hit a
drive of 382 yards on the eighth hole, albeit aided
by a strong wind and frozen, snowless ground.

Travis believed that being ready to play well on the first tee of a
match was key, and once offered this pearl: "Never forget that if
instead of winning the first hole you lose it, two more holes
have to be played and you have to win both before you can
be in the lead; and you are then merely one up when perhaps
you might have been at least two and possibly three up."

In 1914, Travis authored a Glossary of Golf Terms for *The Ameri-can Golfer* magazine, one of the few available to the general public at the time. It included definitions for words such as sclaff [to hit the ground before striking the ball, thus robbing the stroke of a good deal of its strength], foozle [a badly played stroke], and gobble [a putt played with such force that, although it goes into the hole, would otherwise have gone some distance beyond].

Travis's shoe size was seven.

Travis smoked Ricoro Coronas that he ordered in lots of 200 from the United Cigar Stores Company of America at the Flatiron Building in New York City.

In May of 1999, *Golf World* named Travis the second most underrated architect of the twentieth century, noting, "No designer created more ferocious bunkers. See Garden City (in New York) or Hollywood (in New Jersey)."

Donald Ross once said of Travis: "I used to play a great deal with Walter Travis and I watched him get crabbier and crabbier the older he got. He was always a great putter right up to the time he quit the game in disgust, but his long shots became shorter and shorter and he couldn't reconcile himself to his loss of distance."

Travis once wrote to his Uncle John: "I'm quite of your way of thinking with regard to the 18th Amendment [Prohibition]. It is a remarkable thing but I have yet to meet a single man of my acquaintance who is in favor of it."

He received a royalty of 30 cents a copy from the sale of *Practical Golf*.

To family and friends, and especially his wife, Walter John Travis was always known as Jack. Travis called his wife Anne either Nancy or Nan.

Travis charged $125 plus expenses for a one-day inspection, $2,000 to design a nine-hole course, $3,000 for an 18-hole course, and $4,000 for a reversible 18-hole course that could be played in either direction.

Travis frequented many fine hotels during his travels, but his favorites were the Equinox in Manchester, Vermont; the Kirkwood in Camden, South Carolina; the Stevens House in Lake Placid, New York; Royal Poinciana in Palm Beach, Florida; and the Bon-Air Vanderbilt in Augusta, Georgia.

Despite the fact that his son Bartlett was a single digit handicapper for much of his playing career, by his own admission he never beat his father in a round of golf—even when Travis was in his 60s.

The Ekwanok
Country
Club

Manchester-in-the-Mountains
Vermont

Score Card

DIVOTS
It is the duty of every Golfer to
see replaced any turf cut in the
act of play.

1.	1899	Ekwanok	18-hole design	w/John Duncan Dunn
2.	1902	Old Country Club (NLE)	consult	FKA Flushing GC
3.	1906	Garden City	remodel	
4.	1906	Pinehurst No. 2	consult	w/Donald Ross
5.	1907	Salisbury Links	18-hole design	LKA Cherry Valley
6.	1907	Van Cortlandt Park	consult	
7.	1908	Essex County GC	remodel	w/John Duncan Dunn
8.	1908	Poland Spring	consult	
9.	1910	Chevy Chase Club	consult	w/Donald Ross
10.	1911	Youngstown	18-hole design	
11.	1915	Westchester Hills	consult	w/Pete Clark
12.	1916	Columbia	remodel	w/Walter Harban
13.	1916	West Potomac Park	9-hole design	w/Walter Harban
14.	1916	Orchard Park	18-hole design	
15.	1917	Canoe Brook	18-hole design	
16.	1917	Hollywood	18-hole design	
17.	1917	Garden City Country Club	18-hole design	
18.	1917	Pine Valley	consult	w/George Crump
19.	1918	Onondaga	18-hole design	

20.	1918	White Beeches	18-hole design	
21.	1919	Lochmoor	18-hole design	w/John S. Sweeney
22.	1921	Lookout Point	18-hole design	
23.	1921	Cape Arundel	18-hole design	w/John Duncan Dunn
24.	1921	Stafford	18-hole design	
25.	1921	Westchester-Biltmore	36-hole design	LKA Westchester CC
26.	1922	North Jersey	18-hole design	
27.	1922	North Penn Club	18-hole design	LKA Penn Hills
28.	1922	Round Hill	18-hole design	
29.	1923	Cherry Hill	18-hole design	
30.	1923	Kirkwood Links	18-hole design	LKA Camden CC
31.	1923	Oak Ridge (NLE)	18-hole design	
32.	1924	Yahnundasis	27-hole design	(9-hole course NLE)
33.	1924	Yountakah (NLE)	18-hole design	
34.	1924	Milwaukee	18-hole design	Travis design NLE
35.	1924	Augusta	remodel	
36.	1924	CC of New Canaan	remodel	
37.	1924	Louisville	18-hole design, 9-hole remodel	
38.	1924	Philadelphia	consult	

39.	1924	Pasadena	consult
40.	1925	Granliden	9-hole design
41.	1925	CC of Scranton	18-hole design
42.	1926	Grover Cleveland	remodel
43.	1926	Jeykll Island	9-hole design
44.	1927	Sea Island	9-hole design
45.	1927	Equinox	18-hole design
46.	1927	CC of Troy	18-hole design

Dates undetermined:

47.	—	Grand Mere	consult
48.	—	Lakewood	consult
49.	—	Long Vue	consult

FKA: First known as
LKA: Later known as
NLE: No longer exists

Bibliography

Books

Barron, Leonard; *Lawns and How to Make Them, Together with the Proper Keeping of Putting Greens,* New York: Doubleday, Page & Co., 1906.

Behrend, John; *The Amateur,* Worcestershire, England: Grant Books, 1995.

Comstock, Edward Jr., and Edwin B. Bruce; *The Onondaga Golf and Country Club 1898–1998,* Fayetteville, New York, 1998.

Cornish, Geoffrey S. and Ronald E. Whitten; *The Architects of Golf,* New York: Harper Collins, 1993.

D'Agostino, Muriel; *Yahnundasis Golf Club, A Century of Tradition,* New Hartford, New York, 1997.

Elliott, Len and Barbara Kelly; *Who's Who in Golf,* New Rochelle, New York: Arlington House Publishers, 1976.

Fulkerson, Neal and John T. Thacher; *The Garden City Golf Club, Seventy-Fifth Anniversary,* Garden City, 1974.

Gibson, Nevin; *The Encyclopedia of Golf,* New York: A.S. Barnes & Co., 1958.

Gurda, John; *A Sense of Tradition, The Centennial History of the Milwaukee Country Club,* Milwaukee, Wisconsin, 1993.

Gurley, Joseph E.; *Youngstown Country Club; 100 Years of Golfing and Assorted History,* Youngstown, Ohio, 1998

Hecker, Genevieve; *Golf for Women,* New York: The Baker and Taylor Company, 1902.

Hogben, John; *The Golf Craze by Cleeke Shotte, Esq. of Bunker Hill,* Edinburgh, Scotland: T.N. Foulis, 1905.

Hotchkiss, John F.; *500 Years of Golf Balls,* Dubuque, Iowa: Antique Trader Books, 1997.

Hutchinson, Horace G.; *Fifty Years of Golf.* London: Country Life, 1914.

Leach, Henry; *Great Golfers in the Making,* Philadelphia: George W. Jacobs & Co., 1907.

Macdonald, Charles B.; *Scotland's Gift—Golf,* New York: Charles Scribner's Sons, 1928.

Martin, Harold H.; *This Happy Isle,* Sea Island, Georgia, 1978.

Martin, H.B.; *Fifty Years of American Golf,* New York: Dodd, Mead & Co., 1936.

Martin, H.B.; *The Garden City Golf Club Golden Anniversary,* Garden City, 1949.

Matthew, Sidney L.; *Life and Times of Bobby Jones,* Tallahassee, Florida: IQ Press, 1995.

McMahon, Terrance A.; *Country Club of Scranton, A History 1896–1987,* Scranton, Pennsylvania, 1987.

Murdoch, Joseph S.F.; *The Library of Golf 1743–1966,* Detroit: Gale Research Company, 1968.

Newman, Joseph, *The Official Golf Guide for America, 1901,* London: Official Golf Guide Publications, 1902.

Piper, Charles V. and Russell A. Oakley; *Turf for Golf Courses,* New York: Macmillan Company, 1917.

Quirin, Dr. William L.; *Golf Clubs of the MGA,* New York: Golf Magazine Properties, 1997.

Quirin, Dr. William L.; *Hollywood Golf Club, The First Hundred Years,* Virginia Beach, Virginia: The Donning Company, 1998.

Quirin, Dr. William L.; *The Garden City Golf Club, Centennial Anniversary,* Garden City, 1999.

Reynolds, William S.; *The Cherry Hill Club, Ltd. 1922–1997,* Ridgeway, Ontario, Canada, 1997.

Shapiro, Mel; *Golf: A Turn of the Century Treasury,* Secaucus, NJ: Castle Books, 1986.

Stokes, Sydney; *A History of Ekwanok, Commemorating its 75th Anniversary Year,* Manchester, Vermont, 1974.

Taylor, J.H.; *Golf: My Life's Work,* London: Jonathan Cape, 1943.

Tillinghast, A.W.; *Reminiscences of the Links,* Springfield, New Jersey: TreeWolf Productions, 1998.

Travers, Jerome D. and James R. Crowell; *The Fifth Estate,* New York: Alfred A. Knopf, 1926.

Travis, Walter J.; *Practical Golf,* New York: Harper & Brothers Publishing, 1900, 1902, 1909 editions.

Travis, Walter J. and Jack White, *The Art of Putting,* London: Macmillan & Co., 1904.

Tufts, Richard S.; *The Scottish Invasion,* Pinehurst, North Carolina: Pinehurst Publishers, 1962.

USGA Record Book 1895–1971, Far Hills, New Jersey, 1971.

Vardon, Harry: *The Complete Golfer,* New York: Doubleday, Page & Co., 1922.

Wagner, J. Patrick; *White Beeches Golf & Country Club, 75th Anniversary,* Haworth, New Jersey, 1995.

Williams, A.J. *Maldon and the Tarrangower Diggings,* Maldon, Victoria, Australia: The Tarrangower Times, 1987.

Wind, Herbert Warren; *The Story of American Golf,* New York: Simon & Schuster, 1956.

Newspapers:

The New York Times

The New York Sun

The Boston Herald

Magazines:

Golf Illustrated (U.S.)

Golf

The American Golfer

Golf Illustrated (U.K.)

Collier's

Country Life in America

Outing

Harper's Monthly

Munsey's Magazines

The Golfers Magazine

£ s. d.

JU
3
04

Charges
to pay

Tet

at 5.9 .M., Received here at } 5

golf club Sandwich

members of Roya
club send heart

No. of Telegram..........

Office

£ s. d.

Charges
to pay

SAND
44
JU
O

k

at 5.30 .M., Received here at } 8.

Travis Sandwich

Hilton think of
now hearty congra
Sheldon